Legend and Romance, African and European
Volume 2

LEGEND AND ROMANCE,

AFRICAN AND EUROPEAN.

BY RICHARD JOHNS,

LIEUT. ROYAL MARINES.

IN THREE VOLUMES.

VOL. II.

LONDON:

RICHARD BENTLEY, NEW BURLINGTON STREET.

1839.

SEBASTIAN OF PORTUGAL.

SEBASTIAN OF PORTUGAL.

CHAPTER XVIII.

THE HARIFE.

MULEY MOLOCH, whose dethronement of Muley Hamet occasioned Sebastian's expedition to Barbary, had from his youth been more sinned against than sinning. He was the son of Muley Mahomet, Emperor of Fez and Morocco, whom some historians call a wise prince,—a character but vaguely supported by the last act of his life. The subdivision of his kingdom at his death was so indefinitely declared, that Muley Abdallah, his eldest son, choosing to wrest the meaning of his deceased father's will, seized on the whole empire, and would not assign to his brothers, Muley

Moloch and Muley Abdelmumen, any portion of the vast regions which had fallen under his sway: a proceeding diametrically opposed to the known intention of the late Harife. The two brothers, fearing that the deprivation of their share in the dominions of their father, might be followed up by attempts on their lives, fled into Turkey. Here, however, the murderous purpose of the usurper followed them: Muley Moloch escaped by placing himself under the protection of the Sultan Selim; but Muley Abdelmumen, while at prayer in a mosque within the city of Tremessen, was assassinated by an emissary of Muley Hamet,—son to the Emperor Muley Abdallah,—who inherited shortly after, on the death of his father, the two kingdoms of Barbary. Muley Moloch, being made acquainted with these events, determined to regain the throne of his sires, while he avenged the death of a brother by the dethronement of his nephew. The Grand Seignor Amurath, who had then succeeded the Sultan Selim,

afforded him a small detachment of troops as
a nucleus for an army, and embarked them
in two galleys; empowering Moloch to draw
further succour from Algiers, then tributary
to the Porte;—the Dey of which state was, by
the direction of the Sultan, to accompany the
adventurous prince till he was placed on the
throne.

With three thousand arquebusiers, and ten
pieces of artillery, Muley Moloch invaded Fez.
Gathering fresh troops daily from those who
were disaffected to Muley Hamet, he gained
repeated victories over the new Emperor, who
at length, scarcely attempting to compete with
his uncle's increasing army, retired before him.
Finally, after a pitched battle, which for a
while decided the fate of the empire, Muley
Moloch ascended the throne, as Emperor of
Fez and Morocco, while his nephew took re-
fuge in the mountains of Claros, from which
retreat he opened a negotiation with Sebastian
of Portugal, as we have already narrated.

Muley Moloch, to the last, had hoped that the Christians would accept the terms he offered, not from fear, but from a desire to hold friendly relations with all lands;—yet when he heard of the actual landing of Sebastian, rousing like a lion whose strength has not departed from him,—though, had his enemies permitted, willingly would he have remained in his lair,—he prepared himself to oppose the invasion. A reconnaissance of the Christian army by his bastard brother Mahomet, whom he had already declared his heir, was the first operation of the campaign. This, undertaken with the intention of intimidating the invaders, completely failed, as we have just shown, and but for the treachery of Montoyo, the Moors would have been routed with much greater loss than they sustained. In the mean time Moloch continued to advance with a large army, the fidelity of which he ascertained and ensured, by a wise, moderate, and generous policy. Suspecting that some of his troops were favourably disposed towards his nephew, he caused it to be proclaimed that those who chose to side with Muley Hamet and his Christian allies, were at liberty to depart from his army,—a permission their full reliance on the integrity of the Emperor, induced several of his adversary's adherents to accept; and these had safe conduct even to the outposts of the enemy. Still was he suspicious of a large portion of his officers, in consequence of the well-known susceptibility of Mahommedan commanders to bribery:—dreading the effect of Portuguese gold far more than the Christian armament; and to circumvent whatever influence the venality of his captains might induce them to exercise among the men they were accustomed to command, he now changed the distribution of his officers; and by suddenly appointing them to strange corps, broke up any treasonable understanding that might before have existed.

We have not space to enter into one half of

Muley Moloch's judicious arrangements to insure the stability of his throne against the invaders: yet did treachery strike at the heart of the noble Mahommedan; from what quarter is unknown; though suspicion pointed to Muley Hamet as the instigator of the deed. Moloch had made his first encampment at Tremesenal, on the direct road to Alcazarquiver, and here there is little doubt poison, slow but deadly in its effects, was administered to him: yet the gallant spirit of the Emperor succumbed not to the pangs which racked his frame. Fresh troops continued to arrive,—they were officered and organised by his direction; scouts and spies from the Christian camp he personally interrogated; and by frequent communications with his chiefs, through their means, he became the soul of his vast army,—instilling energy and order into the heterogeneous materials of which it was composed.

Gorgeous were the hangings of Muley Moloch's pavilion, — silken draperies fell in soft folds, brilliant as if woven from the emerald's rays ;—cords wrought of shredded gold, rather than golden thread, were suspended in festoons around ; while fringe of bullion weighed the curtains to the earth. The exterior of the tent, though flaunting in scarlet and gold, was of more durable material ; and before the principal entrance proudly stood the standard of the crescent, as if daring the Christian invader to the assault ; four smaller flags marking the angles of the canvass walls.

We have already introduced Muley Moloch to the reader, by the fairest record whereby man can judge of man—his deeds. We would fain not draw back a curtain of that tent which hides suffering humanity,—the quenching of the light of life, the last thread unravelling of that clue of destiny which hath conducted from the cradle to the grave—but it must be ; —for honourable as had been the career of the Harife, it might truly be said of him, " nothing in his life became him like the leaving it ;" and it is necessary for the elucidation of our story, that we should linger by the departing hero, demanding for him the sympathy of generous hearts.

On a large couch, or divan, which occupied one whole side of an inner compartment, appertaining to the pavilion,—hidden from the eye of all except his chosen officers,—lay Muley Moloch. He was dying from a disorder which produced the most excruciating tortures, and consequent prostration of strength; but the mind was unconquered by disease. The ethereal essence seemed to spurn the vile body that trammelled it with its petty troubles, when a despotic murderer claimed a throne as a theatre for his crimes,—an invader was on the shores of Morocco,—an empire to be lost or won. Almost writhing with agony, the Harife was yet giving orders to his generals;—even at intervals sketching with his own hand plans of operation, and in all showing powers of intellect which appeared strengthened and purified as the fires of disease consumed its clayey crucible.

" I have arranged these matters now, and shall feel more at mine ease," said the monarch, addressing his officers, as he passed a scroll, which had for some time engaged his attention, to Latava, a renegade Genoese, his favourite attendant: " the council is dissolved: by, the mercy of Allah I would sleep!" and Moloch, waiving his dismissal to the surrounding chiefs, reclined on the cushions placed for his support. " Hold!" cried the Moorish King,—pushing aside Latava, who was obsequiously busying himself about the couch, and once more nerving himself for exertion. " I said that I would examine those Christian youths, brought in by the Arab scouts. Emirs and chiefs, I require not your attendance."

When the grave, turbaned conclave had gone forth, Muley Moloch, who was unable to walk, caused himself to be conveyed to an outer division of the pavilion by two strong mutes,

preceded by Latava, the Renegade having
previously ascertained that no stranger would
behold the transmission of the sufferer from
one apartment to the other. Here, seated on a
divan, unsupported, and every feature schooled into subjection, that the agony he endured
might not be apparent, he gave orders for the
admission of the captives. The reader will
readily imagine these were no other than Beatrice and Zuma. After having been overtaken
and captured, without further adventure they
had been brought to the Moorish camp, and
now stood trembling before Muley Moloch.
In the noble character of features, open brow,
and graceful bearing of the Harife, there was
more to create confidence than is generally to
be remarked in the personal characteristics of
a Mahommedan ruler; whose frown is, meta-
phorically, death. The eyes of the disguised
girls were no sooner raised to meet the inquir-
ing gaze of the Moorish monarch, than half
their fears subsided. No one was in attendance

but the Renegade, who occasionally acted as interpreter, though, in this case, his royal master needed not his services : the intimate connexion between the Moors and the Portuguese had induced a prince of Moloch's intelligence to make himself acquainted with their language.

" I am given to understand that you are servitors belonging to a noble of Portugal," said the Harife, after he had for some time contemplated his captives. " Allah grant that Sebastian brings chiefs who have hardier followers than these to battle on the shores of Morocco ; or I have stirred up my kingdom to resist an army of boys whom our schoolmen might have whipped into subjection. There will be no triumph in such victory. Speak —tell me why ye should not be stript, manacled, and made to work in the camp; yourselves enslaved ' who, came to make us slaves — to dictate to Morocco and Morocco's Emperor !"

Muley Moloch had raised his voice as he poured forth the scornful termination of this appalling inquiry. The captives answered not, but all their bitterest fears returning, they withdrew their gaze from the now excited monarch, and looked at each other. Beatrice burst into tears, an example Zuma was not long in following; while the secret of their sex was at once disclosed to the experienced eye of Muley Moloch, who beckoned their nearer approach. The girls glanced behind them, almost expecting that the messengers of the King's imperious will were ready to drag them forth. Timidly did they draw near to the divan which Beatrice was the first to reach. Placing his withered hand on her glowing cheek, the Harife smiled as he parted her long hair.

" What! worse indignity to be offered our warriors ;—are Portuguese maidens come to war with us? And thou, too," continued Moloch, turning to Zuma,—" who seemest more like a

daughter of our land than a Christian girl,—
hast for some strange cause unsexed thyself to
be a greater riddle."

" I go to my betrothed in the camp of Sebastian," said Beatrice, at length gaining utterance, and aware that further concealment
would be vain.

" And I "—here Zuma paused, and the deep
crimson mounted to her brow.

" Have no betrothed, but would fain seek
one," interrupted Moloch, who read not the
poor girl's conscious blushes aright. " The time
is past with me when thou mightest have graced
my harem—my bride now is glory, and our
bridal bed shall be the tomb. But Allah is
good—Muley Moloch will be victorious ere he
dies."

At this moment the curtain of the pavilion
was moved ; the Renegade hastened to demand
the cause, and announced to the monarch that
a Portuguese, unarmed, and bearing a flag of

truce, had delivered himself up at one of the advanced posts, demanding an audience of the Emperor on matters of the deepest import.

" Admit him instantly,"—replied the Harife: —" let him be searched that he bear not concealed weapons ;—we will see him, and alone. For you, Christian maidens, I will hear what you have to communicate when I have dismissed your countryman.   Within that curtain you may bestow yourselves, and leave us to our conference."

Glad to escape from an interview which had been sufficiently distressing,—though their fears of actual outrage had much subsided by Muley Moloch's bland and almost friendly bearing after the discovery of their sex,—Beatrice and Zuma passed through an opening in the drapery, and found themselves in a small apartment, divided but by silken hangings from the divan chamber. The voice of Christovao sounded on the ear of the Moorish girl ere she had drawn the curtain of the tent ; motionless—in

the same position as when those well-known accents had reached her,—she clung to the long
folds within her grasp, and listened, as if spell-
bound, to the conference between Muley Moloch and the traitor Montoyo. Ere the first
shock of discovering in Christovao a betrayer
of his King,—for such his appearance in the
Moorish camp betokened him,—allowed Zuma
to understand what was the nature of his communication, the Marquis had professed great
influence in Sebastian's councils, and proposed
to render this influence available in aiding the
destruction of the Christian army.

" And you offer to hasten the advance of the
invaders, regularly communicate their movements, and ensure my speedily bringing them
to action ?" said Muley Moloch in reply to the
offers of service which had fallen from Christovao.

" It is exactly what I propose, sire," rejoined the Marquis ; " and that you may put faith
in my professions of service, I avow myself the

author of those letters which have twice given information of Sebastian's intended operations ; —and I would further state, it was by my instrumentality the Moorish cavalry were allowed to retreat unopposed when they had failed in their reconnaissance," continued the Marquis, handing duplicates of the traitorous despatches, together with the minutes of his new proposal to Muley Moloch.

While Zuma had been eagerly gathering the import of this interview, Beatrice more than once entreated her to say what had so blanched her cheek, and still engaged her fixed attention. An admonitory " Hush"—" move not"—and a hurried wave of the hand, had been the only answer to these inquiries ; nor had the Donna even approached the screen where Zuma stood in breathless agitation, and she consequently knew not the vicinage of her brother. The moment Montoyo presented the documents to Muley Moloch, who shrunk from contact with the traitor though he accepted his treason, Beatrice, to her great alarm, beheld Zuma dart through the curtained partition—her wild scream ringing through the pavilion—" Christovao, Christovao ! betray not thy King and country." The Donna, controlling her anxious fears, proceeded no further than the position quitted by her friend, from whence, herself unobserved, she beheld Zuma clinging to Christovao, and attempting to take the scroll from his hand, which she,—in her imperfect perception of the matter in progress,—imagined comprised within itself mischief to Sebastian, and degradation to Montoyo in betraying him.

Christovao's astonishment at the unexpected appearance of Zuma for a moment absorbed every other feeling. He then endeavoured to soothe the excited girl by his caresses, and looked significantly towards Muley Moloch, who was not the least surprised of the party at the scene before him. The Harife clapped his hands, and called aloud, on which the Renegade appeared, attended by two mutes.

" Remove the captives, Latava : we would be alone : and see ! one of them has intruded on our privacy."

Thus addressed by his royal master, the Genoese approached Zuma, and on his making a sign to the eunuchs, they drew aside the curtains, and led Beatrice forth from the tent. Hurriedly the Donna passed, anxious to escape the observation of her brother ; and Christovao, who was engaged in answering the Moorish girl's continued appeals,— " Why wrong the confidence of thy King ? — why betray thy countrymen to slaughter ?" — caught but a glance of the retreating form. Ever ready to suspect her he had so often wronged by jealous suspicions, his countenance fell.

" You have a companion, Zuma," said the Marquis gravely.

" And we have matters that were better discussed at once," sternly interrupted Muley Moloch : " this is no hour for love or child's play : Latava, take her from the tent."

"I may be permitted to ransom that maiden, —at least to see her again,"—said the Marquis inquiringly, as Zuma was led away by the Renegade, her tears alone answering Christovao's cold look of distrust.

" Ransom her thou mayest not, Senhor ; and thy sight of her must be brief, for in less than half an hour thou shalt quit the Moorish camp. By the first of these papers I perceive that thou are to be trusted in thy treason: frown not," exclaimed the Harife ; " 'tis well we should speak plainly, the better to understand each other ;—the second document proposes that, in consideration of the Christian army's movements being duly communicated to us, and Sebastian speedily induced to give us battle,— with other aids which circumstances may give thee power to afford the cause of Morocco,— I am to guarantee thy free ransom, if taken, together with protection, shouldst thou stay in Barbary,—or, at thy pleasure, safe passage to Portugal, with secrecy as to thy treason.—Am I not right, Elchie ?"

"It is not treason, monarch," exclaimed Christovao; "by Heaven! I only—"

"Betray thy King,"—again interrupted Muley Moloch, faintly smiling: "well! we quarrel not for terms. The poison traitors drugged me with, still burns in every vein, and I must fight mine enemies with the treachery they have taught me. Require ye no reward? —Gold, Marquis, gold, the Christian's god?"

"Muley Moloch!" sternly pronounced Christovao, "I came not here to listen to thy taunts, and, but that my reward is far beyond the treasure of thine empire,—thou mightest tear me limb from limb by Arab horses, ere I would make the crescent triumph o'er the cross! Revenge, revenge for deeply-seated wrongs!— this, monarch, thou canst give me in Sebastian's fall. I demand no more save secrecy, and ransom for that maiden."

He paused hesitatingly, and then resumed. "Might I ask who is her fellow captive?"

"I know not, Elchie; thou hadst better in-

quire of the maiden : a few minutes' converse
with her may be thine, though nought can
ransom her but thy fidelity to Muley Moloch.
She is our hostage; and if thou fearest the
other captive may betray thee, know that they
both remain our prisoners.   Nay, no more."

The Marquis again essayed to speak, but
the Harife would not listen to him.

" Our conference has lasted through its
purpose.—It is enough."   And summoning the
Renegade, he dismissed Montoyo, whose daring
spirit had never till then been taught thus to
succumb; so completely had he, by the end of
that interview, lost the proud bearing of the
man in the traitor.

Within an adjoining tent he was permitted
to see Zuma.

" Christovao," reproachfully demanded the
Moorish girl, " why is our meeting to be
robbed of half its joy ?   Why art thou here ?
Thou canst not even ransom me."

" Thou hast said truly," moodily replied the

Marquis. " But the youth, thy fellow page, will make thee all amends ;"—then watching the countenance of Zuma for a moment, he violently continued — " Tell me at once, false woman ! if thy love has cooled —hast found another lover ?"

" Shame, shame, Christovao !" sobbed the hapless girl ; " whom have I loved but thee ?"

" The stranger ! the stranger !" exclaimed the incensed Marquis. " Him of the grey and black jerkin, who doubtless came with thee from Portugal."

" My brother came with me from the Tagus," evasively answered Zuma. " The other I know not."

" Plague on thy lying tongue ! Wouldst have me hate thee ? Dost thou love this other ? See ! I am warned to quit the camp. Speak ! or never, never more behold Christovao De Montoyo."

" Spare me, oh ! spare me !" cried Zuma as she followed the Marquis to the door of the tent. " Holy Saints of Heaven ! you will not go in anger.   Say only you will not harm her ? —It is Beatrice."

The rage of Christovao was for the moment so intense that it found no utterance in words. He spurned Zuma as she clung to him, and rushed towards the pavilion of Muley Moloch to demand his sister ; but here his impetuous course was arrested. The Harife slept. Forced back by the guards, the Marquis would again have returned to Zuma, that he might vent on her the first burst of his passion, and then re-concile himself, as was his wont, to one in whom he could forgive all save the semblance of diminished affection. The Moorish soldiers listened not to his solicitations—he was dis-missed the camp.

CHAPTER XIX.

THE KINSMEN.

WE must now conduct our reader to a tent pitched in a desert tract of country, not more than a mile from the spot where the encounter with Muley Moloch's Arab scouts separated Zadig from Beatrice and Zuma.

" Thou feelest better, my son," said Abdallah, the guide, who, with the young Moor, was the only inhabitant of the rude shelter which had been their place of abode for several days.

Zadig was lying on a couch, formed by the furniture of two horses which were stabled in an opposite corner of the tent ; and his uncle, for such was the relationship of the guide to his patient, had been administering to him a copious bowl of camel's milk, procured from a neighbouring Dowar.

" The fever hath left me, and the wound is healing," slowly answered the young Moor, " but where is the strength that once lived in these sinews? I lift my arm, and it falls as though it had ceased to do my bidding. Raise me, mine uncle, for thus I call thee, though I know not why ;—there—I breathe more freely. Oh ! that strength would come !—Celestial signs of my nativity ! I know thou hast promised ill in all the Houses of my pilgrimage, but is it thus my flame of life must perish—ground to the dust—quenched amid desert sands?"

" Thy strength will yet return," replied Abdallah, seating himself by Zadig, who, feeling his weakness in a more upright position, had impatiently fallen back again on his couch, and buried his face in the mat which formed his pillow. " Thou shalt soon follow the maiden who hath fashioned the visions of thy fever. Alas! that the son of my brother should so madly love a Christian girl. Now thou didst address her as a Peri bearing thee to bliss — now as thine evil genius offering thee a crystal bowl of luscious wine with poison in the dregs;—and then thou didst call her thy sister, and besought her not to sacrifice a heart so young, so pure, to one thou saidst was stern and proud. Thou didst name him Christovao."

" There were two maidens, father, and they mingled in my dreams," answered Zadig. " One was indeed my sister, and thy brother's child; protected, loved, and cherished by the Christian Donna: but tell me how comes this strange relationship ?"

" It is not strange, Zadig. I and thy father were the only sons of a Beréber, — a dweller in the mountains Djibbel Habeeb, — who having in the wars waged by Muley Abdelmelech, when he united the kingdoms of

Barbary, done good service for the Harife, was by him made alcaydes of Tetuan. At the desire of an elder brother of my father, who was the Sheik of our tribe, I was left on Djibbel Habeeb; for Allah had then shut the wombs of Achmet's harem, and the sons of his strength, like saplings that wither ere the parent root decays, had gone down to the cave where the bones of their father had not yet come. Thus said the old Sheik to his kinsman departing from him. 'Leave Abdallah with me, for no male of my race stands in my presence, and our tribe hath long been ruled by a chief from the loins of our fathers. Even now the Angel Azrael waits for me. I go down to the cave of Kehaya, and thy son shall sit in my place;—the Berēbers shall obey him, and he will lead them to the plunder of the plains.' So thy father journeyed to the town of Tetuan, which he ruled for the Harife when thy grand-sire died, and I saw not often the brother of my youth. Then came the army of the Chris-

tians like the blast of the Simoom. Thy sir
was slain, and his children led into a strang
land. Achmet died, ripe of years, and I wa
obeyed in the huts and in the tents of ou
tribe : but a voice came to me in the mour
tain and followed me in the desert — it neithe
slumbered nor slept—it was the cry of the Pro
phet to those whom he chooseth to approac
the spiritual *Kaaba.* No one knows thos
words but he to whom the Prophet hath spoke
them. I obeyed. Thus have I been twice t
Mecca, and become a wanderer, dwelling a
often in the tents of the Bedouins as in th
mountains of Djibbel Habeeb ; for I love a
men who love Mahommed, and live not i
cities, and all men reverence me and call m
Augur. Now have I told Zadig, the son c
my brother, why I have cried unto him, Lo
thou art my kinsman : and I would say unt
thee, even as Achmet said to me in year
gone by,—Make thy home in the land whic

to thee, — ay, even will I do good to those whom Zadig, my son, doth love."

" And this is our relationship," said Zadig musingly : " then, if so seldom thou didst visit us in Tetuan, how knewest thou the stranger Moor, returning from a foreign land, was the son of thy brother ? I call myself a Moor in right of my mother's race: I have been a slave, and no longer claim to be a Berēber."

" Because thy name, thy features, spoke to me of thy father ; and I had seen thee as a child, ere thou wert led into captivity. She whom thou callest Zuma, I knew not,—the mention of her birth had never reached mine ears. I saw thee—it was enough,—I provided thee with horses,—and desiring to know why Zadig the Berēber journeyed with Christian youths, offered to be thy guide. Thou knowest the rest. I set not the Arabs on, but would have taken thee even to Sebastian's camp. I am received there without suspicion, for Muley Hamet knows me for a man too wearied of

Moorish politics to lend mine aid to either party. But what saith my son ?—will he dwell with the brother of his father ?"

" If thou swearest to me that thou wilt indeed do good unto those I love — if thou wilt truly serve yon maiden in any danger that may threaten, till the moon which is now at its full doth wane and grow again, then will I make my home with thee in the land where I was born;—though I may go away for a while, yet will I return to thee."

" I swear to thee," solemnly replied Abdallah. " The Donna hath protected a daughter of our race, and I will be her safeguard. My oath is not a light one, made to be recalled, for I am making up my account with man, and I will deal justly with thee. If I have days to come, let them be pure of sin,— youth lives unto this world,—but age hath its world beyond the grave. How often we give to Allah the thin runnings of our blood,—the nerves relaxed in vigour, and the frame worn

by the toils of our departed days—such are our
offerings ;—but the lust of life,—the might,—
the youthful swelling of our veins, these are
the world's.   Oh ! it would seem as if the gate
which leads to the eternal bowers of bliss,
would not give entrance to the soul till purified of grosser matter.   The young may
babble about creeds, and ere the chanted
prayer, and song of adoration shall have passed
their lips, the stag eyes of a mistress claims
the harmony that was upraised to heaven.
The young may talk of death,—may brave it
in the field,—or when they have found the worm
of disappointment concealed within the ripe
fruit of their hope, and bitterness doth gush
upon the palate where only sweets had flowed
—they then may call for death, but 'tis an idle
mockery.   Its icy touch agrees not with the
powers of life : there comes an awful struggle,
and the angel of the dark valley receives no
welcome.   The old can make death familiar
as a friend, and look for it as the Arab waits to

greet the traveller whose course along the desert he hath watched for hours. Now a cloud rising in the far distance,—now a speck, a moving body,—now 'tis man and steed,—the long expected hath arrived, and see, an open tent awaits him: such is death to me; I seek it not, but calmly wait its coming."

" The aged or the young must each work out his destiny," muttered Zadig, who had listened to the old man till slumber crept upon him, and when Abdallah turned to renew his homily, he found the young Moor stretched on his couch asleep.

In a few days Zadig had recovered sufficient strength to undertake the proposed journey, in search of his companions. His kinsman, so he but wandered, cared little in what direction it might be ; and he had, moreover, sworn to the impassioned Moor that he would protect the Donna Beatrice; and no one could better afford this protection, for he was held in the odour of sanctity, not only among the Berēbers, but the Bedouins, and could, at his beck, have thrown a powerful subsidy of men into the ranks of either of the parties now contending for the empire, drawn from many a wandering tribe, who, at present, preferred plundering both armies to siding with either one against the other, which would have materially reduced their perquisites.

Advice had reached the kinsmen, that Muley Moloch, after having broken up his camp at Tremesenal, had re-formed it within a few miles of Alcazarquiver: this information was procured from the Arab scouts who, on the same mission as the party which had captured the Senhoras, kept up a constant communication with the coast, to acquaint the Moorish Emperor of any reinforcements arriving from Europe to swell the Christian army. Zadig likewise ascertained from the same source, that two youths were held hostages in the camp, on some account which was not generally divined; and that a Portuguese Elche had claimed them both as his pages, but, after having had a long audience with Muley Moloch, his anxious desire to ransom the darker of the two was refused. They consequently both remained in the power of the Moors, and were held in great consideration by the Emperor; rode constantly by his litter, and resided in a tent allotted to them, near the royal pavilion.

"It is strange that the Marquis Montoyo cares not to ransom Beatrice," said Zadig, turning to his kinsman, with whom he was eating his last meal in the Arab tent, ere they departed on their journey.

" I see nothing strange in this, my son," answered Abdallah. " Thou hast told me thy fears that the rose of our race found favour in the eyes of the proud Portuguese — Allah forbid that she hath wasted her bloom on the Christian dog. Said not the man, who was drinking of our cup but now, that the Elche called them his pages?"

" Even so, mine uncle," said Zadig; " and I know not who would have cared to ransom either of the maidens, save the Marquis de Montoyo, unless it be a Senhor Abrantes: but he had surely sought to release Beatrice."

The young Moor sighed deeply.

" Montoyo!" rejoined Abdallah, " there was a Christian Elche of that name, who, when I was at Arzilla, asked me, if in a ship that had of late arrived at Tangiers, from whence I came, there was not a page belonging to his retinue. I asked him to describe the youth, and then he talked of lustrous eyes, and ruby lips, till I turned from him, saying, thou hast a leman in her thou callest a page — I pander not to lust."

" Old man! thou sayest not Christovao spoke thus of my sister?" exclaimed Zadig.

" I say that a Christian Elche spoke thus of a page whom he expected from the Tagus; he was not called Christovao, in my hearing."

" 'Tis plain, too plain," sorrowfully said the young Moor; " but for this he dies. Kinsman, I swear to thee,"—and Zadig raised his voice, grasping the hand of Abdallah with a

force that told little of his recent weakness;—
" I swear to thee, this Portuguese shall wed
my sister or die."

" 'Tis time, then, we should be on our barbs,
or ere we reach the camp the armies may have
met,—but few of Lusitania's nobles will wear
a marriage robe when Muley Moloch has once
given them battle."

" Kinsman, I would long ere this have departed," responded Zadig, busying himself with
the trappings of his horse, " but thou wouldst
wait to see those scouts."

" And was it not well I did ?" asked Abdallah; " or might we not have journeyed to
Tremesenal ?"

Zadig and the old Marabout now set forward
on their way to the camp. They travelled the
greater portion of that night, and after a few
hours' rest again proceeded, but they reached
not the Moorish encampment till the army of

CHAPTER XX.

TREASON.

Latava, to whom the sex of the pretended pages was well known, while he beheld the glowing charms of Zuma with indifference, became deeply enamoured of the Donna Beatrice. She reminded him of woman's dazzling beauty in the land of his birth: but did the recollection of Genoa soften the stern renegade? No—it served rather to inflame his desire for present enjoyment, by recalling the memory of days when love, even to Latava, was virtue, and the smile of beauty the willing tribute of requited affection. Now the slavish adulation of his harem palled him.

" What then," argued Latava to himself, as

he again paced his tent from whence he had just watched the Senhoras pass toward Muley Moloch's pavilion,—" I have seen love bartered for in Europe. Position, jewels, gold, will buy the heart, or what will suit our purpose just as well, the heart's consent to sell the willing charms. I should pay highly now, methinks," exclaimed the Renegade, as with a laugh he passed his hand over his scarred though once handsome features. Again he commenced a commune with his thoughts. " Gold will not purchase her — she loves another too; and Muley Moloch must play the hero, and be the guardian of this masquerader. She shall be mine," muttered the Renegade, between his teeth. " How now !" exclaimed he, turning to a soldier who had just entered the tent, " has the night-watch been set ?"

" It has, Elche," answered the Mahommedan ; " and again the Christian, who was yesterday in the camp, has approached the outposts. He sends this to you."

The Renegade impatiently received from the bearer a scroll curiously sealed, and demanded who waited his relpy.

"Two strangers came to the outpost, Elche."

"Two!" shouted Latava, giving way to a violence which was common to his perturbed spirit. "Two, liar?"—and he struck the soldier with the stock of his pistol. "Take that, and learn thy duty better; thou saidst but one a moment since."

The man received the blow on his shoulder which had just escaped his head, and staggered to the centre pole of the marquee, while the fiery glance that darted from his eyes was instantly hidden by the drooping of the eyelids as he replied,—

"The Elche has the life of his slave; as Allah lives I lied not—the Christian came with the packet, and an Arab came with him. The Christian departed, and the Arab remains for an answer."

"Thou mightest have said all this before,"

rejoined the Renegade, carelessly waving his hand to the soldier, who submissively went forth from the tent.

Latava, as the favoured general of Muley Moloch, held the lives of the inferior soldiery in his power; but the Mahommedan he struck registered that blow, and would wait but opportunity for its repayment. The Renegade opened the packet, which contained a communication from Christovao, in the following terms:

" The Christian Elche who had audience of the Emperor of Fez and Morocco, thus writes to the chosen officer of Muley Moloch—whom may Allah preserve, and lead to victory!— It is in friendship to the brave Latava, and in consequence of an agreement for mutual benefit between the Emperor and the Christian Elche, that certain intentions on the part of Dom Sebastian are made known to thee. The Portuguese King hath declared it his fixed purpose, in the event of conquest, to extirpate the Europeans who, under adverse circumstances, have

taken service beneath the standard of the crescent, and accepted the faith of Mahommed.
This being just announced in council, thy
friend informs thee of it, hoping its sole effect
may be to render the parties named for extir-
pation firm to the cause of Muley Moloch.
The writer of this letter would fain ask the
brave Latava to use interest with the Emperor,
that his pages may be given in charge to
the Arab who awaits at the Moorish outpost. Services effected, and still in progress for
the advancement of the just cause, without
reference to the appeals of country or religion,
may demand this reward; and the noble Latava will not refuse to forward the claims of
his friend, the Christian Elche."

"The Christian Elche may find other medium of communication with Muley Moloch,"
said the Renegade as he crushed the paper in
his hand. "Yet would I willingly share these
servitors with the Portuguese."

Calling for writing materials, he immediately

answered the letter of the Marquis de Montoyo, by declaring his knowledge of the real sex of the disguised Senhoras, and in confidence offering his services to effect the escape of Zuma, if Beatrice were to be his reward, whatever result might attend the contest for the throne of Fez and Morocco. This was covertly making a treaty with the unknown Christian Elche, and might be far from agreeable to Muley Moloch. Thus Latava, jealous of trusting another, rode to the outpost, where he committed the return packet to the hands of the Arab, Selim, who had become Montoyo's messenger of treason.

When the Marquis received this communication, he was again about to visit the Moorish encampment. The knowledge Dom Christovao had obtained of Muley Moloch's anxiety to give the Christians battle while life was yet allowed him, made the arch-traitor look with an eye of alarm at the present strong position of Sebastian's forces. The King of Portugal

had passed the river El M'Hazen, which is a
branch of the L'Khos, and there forms a delta
with the main stream : his advanced columns
were opposed by the Moorish horse, but he
had succeeded in gaining the plains of Alcazarquiver.   Here Dom Duarte Meneyes, who, in-
dependent of his other offices under Sebastian,
from his knowledge of the country was chosen
chief engineer and quarter-master general, en-
camped the Christians so advantageously, that
while both flanks were protected by the junc-
tion of the rivers, intrenching their front would
enable them effectually to resist an army even
numerous as the Mahommedan.   Doffing the
disguise he wore when visiting the Moorish
camp, the Marquis had taken an early opportunity of presenting himself before the King.
Sebastian was alone : it might even have been
supposed that his guardian angel had departed
from him, for the young monarch, who was
preparing memoranda wherewith to guide the

morning's council, was induced by the wily Marquis to rescind the order for its assembling. Montoyo represented that the Moors ascribed the inactivity of Sebastian to sudden intimidation, and this was in itself enough to fire his daring spirit ; but his traitorous adviser had yet another argument, which he failed not to use with his royal master. He represented the insufficiency of provision in the camp, should they be besieged in their present position, and pictured the disgrace of being obliged to make terms with the infidels.

"What need have I to summon a council but to determine the plan of attack?" said the enthusiastic monarch. "It would but delay our advance to the field of that glorious fight in which I feel imperatively called on to be the assailant. On the battle-plain will I gather my generals around me. Yes! to-morrow shall behold the triumph of the Cross over the infidels."

Montoyo, after remaining with Sebastian

until he was secure that no other adviser would
be admitted, the King having retired to his
couch, was about to seek an interview with
Muley Moloch, for the purpose of communicating the probable events of the morrow,
when Selim placed in his hands the Renegade's
letter.   Indignant at the proposal it contained,
the Marquis still determined on returning an
apparent assent, which he immediately committed to writing; and fearing Latava might
not be in attendance on the Moorish monarch
at the late hour wherein it was necessary
for him to demand an audience, he commanded the Arab to convey his present, after
the manner of his former communication.
Christovao's self-gratulation at the successful
progress of his treason, had induced him to
put much dependance on his powers of dissi-
mulation.   He wrote that Beatrice should become Latava's wife immediately she was freely
her brother's to bestow; yet he looked forward
with confidence to a speedy opportunity of

breaking faith in this matter, when Latava's interest with the Harife had gained the liberation of the two Senhoras.

But the Renegade, after having despatched his letter to the brother of Beatrice, had determined on a different plan of action, more in unison with his fiery and impatient nature. When the Marquis was permitted a midnight audience of Muley Moloch, the Genoese was engaged conferring with a few chosen followers devoted to his service; and had given them directions that whenever the expected action might take place, an abduction of Beatrice from the protection of the Emperor should be attempted. In the confusion of the fight the Donna was to be borne where she would be at the mercy of her captor.

Muley Moloch's reception of Montoyo was far from gracious, for he could not but scorn the traitor he made his instrument. A languid smile passed across the countenance of the Moorish hero, as the Marquis declared Sebastian's determination of leaving his position, and advancing further into the plains.

"Thou hast done me service in this matter, Elche," said the Harife; "bethink thee once more of thy reward."

"The liberation of the damsels," eagerly responded Montoyo.

"No! they are our hostages. Would that I might pay thee with gold. I like not obligations to such as thou art." The Marquis bit his lip in silence, as Muley Moloch continued to address him.

"I give not up my captives till thou hast proved thy fidelity. When the battle of the morrow is decided, should they choose the guardianship of the Marquis de Montoyo, in preference to remaining with Muley Moloch, they shall be delivered to thee. Should either of the damsels claim more unconditional freedom, she shall be conducted even to the gates of Lisboa, controlled but by her own free choice."

The Harife's manner was too gravely imperious to admit of Montoyo's disputing his
pleasure : he begged, however, that it might
be permitted him to see the Donnas; a favour
which was granted with a reservation, that if,
on their being sent for, either of the hostages
declined an interview with him, their royal
guardian would not allow her to be distressed
by his presence.

It was apparent to the Marquis that Beatrice had besought the Emperor to protect her
against him, and after much fruitless solici-
tation, he was obliged to submit. The Donna
refused to attend his bidding; and Zuma,
during her short communication with him, listened in terror to his threats of vengeance on
his sister, for what he termed her contumacy
in appealing to an infidel for aid in opposing
him, rather than bow in proper subjection
to her natural guardian.

" She shall suffer for it. Whatever may be
the result of the coming battle, she shall not

escape me," exclaimed Christovao, as he took leave of Zuma. "And tremble for thyself, girl, if thou dost again thwart my purpose."

The Marquis quitted the camp, and Zuma returned to the tent allotted to the pretended pages, which was not far from the pavilion of Muley Moloch, who looked on them less as hostages for the performance of Christovao's treachery, than as forlorn damsels whose only connection appeared so little worthy of protecting them, that they enlisted his kindest regard at a moment when weightier matters might be supposed to have fully occupied his attention. Generous feelings, be they intellectual or animal, as some would fain persuade us, certainly appear instinctive in many natures. The education of a Harem, his sufferings from the early oppression of his brother—and the oppressed too often becomes in turn the tyrant—his despotic and extensive rule, the wrongs which had been heaped on him, the power he had to avenge them,—an invader in his kingdom, and the poison of a traitor gnawing at his heart, could not make Muley Moloch otherwise than generous in peace, and in war a hero. No; the Moorish Emperor was naturally and philosophically a noble character. We will leave it for others to determine how far this may have arisen from developement of brain, or powers of digestion. It is not often our pen runs away with us in such digressions, and we will once more approach the tent which contains Beatrice and Zuma.

The morning of the fatal battle of Alcazarquiver had arrived. The bride of Sebastian slept: the Moorish girl watched by her side. The grey light of morning was throwing its feeble ray over the couch of Beatrice; and Zuma, who had passed an almost sleepless night, after her interview with Christovao, sorrowfully regarded her friend. The words of dark meaning which had escaped the infuriated Marquis occupied her thoughts as she sat by the side of Beatrice. But she feared not for herself; her alarm was for the unhappy sister of Montoyo.

"He means to seize her in the confusion of the fight, and bear her away—perhaps return her to that hateful convent. Oh, that I might rescue her! I have again betrayed Beatrice by informing her brother she was my companion;— oh, that I might take her place in captivity! It would be but for a short time; Christovao would soon discover who was in his power—I, who have long been subject to his will—he would be angry, but his anger never continues with *me*. He loves me—we should again be re- conciled; and Beatrice, if the arms of Sebas- tian be successful, would have time to seek his protection, and if not, she could remain under the guardianship of the noble Muley Moloch;—anything would be better than her falling into the hands of Christovao."

While Zuma thus silently communed with herself, the vest and tunic, which Beatrice the preceding night had thrown on her couch, caught the attention of the Moorish girl. The feasibility of turning on herself the catastrophe, whatever it might be, which threatened her friend, by assuming these garments, suddenly struck her; and ere Beatrice awoke, Zuma was arrayed in the grey and black dress, leaving her own crimson costume in exchange, and was looking forth into the camp, where all was now in the hurry of preparation for the expected action: Muley Moloch having acquainted his chiefs with the probability of the Christians advancing, it being his intention, immediately a movement was apparent among Sebastian's forces, that the Mahommedans should offer them battle on the plains of Alcazarquiver.

The inquiry of Beatrice, demanding the cause of this exchange of attire, Zuma lightly answered, attributing it to a caprice of the moment, rather than enter into into a detail of Christovao's threatenings, and her intention of braving the result : the Donna might otherwise have opposed her friend's risking an unknown danger in her behalf; for Beatrice, though painfully surprised at the understanding lately so apparent between the Moorish girl and her brother, knew not the hapless position of Zuma with regard to Christovao, which from her very dependence on his affection enabled her to avert his anger. A messenger from the Emperor, demanding their immediate attendance in the royal pavilion, where the Senhoras frequently took their repast, prevented further debate on the subject. Coffee and a light refection awaited them, but they saw not Muley Moloch till they were summoned to take up their position on either side the litter of the Monarch. Two small barbs, elegantly caparisoned, bore the disguised maidens, who, the Moorish army being now in motion, tremblingly regarded the array of war around them.

CHAPTER XXI.

THE BATTLE.

On the morning which decided the fate of the African expedition, Sebastian, to the surprise of his generals, announced his intention of advancing on the enemy. In vain his faithful officers remonstrated with him on the rashness of giving up their present advantageous position. The Marquis de Montoyo had already steeled his royal master against their arguments. The council which had assembled, rather than been summoned, was dismissed by the impetuous King; but several of his faithful nobles again sought his presence. The excitement occasioned by opposition to his inclinations had in some degree passed, and Montoyo, who was

then in the tent of audience, failed not to perceive that he listened dispassionately to their
opinions.   Muley Hamet, too, was among those
who strongly recommended that the Christian
army should remain inactive; but Sebastian
had at length begun to suspect his motives,—
information having reached the camp that Muley Moloch was sinking fast.   One point only
did the King of Portugal seem inclined to
concede to the importunities of his noble
advisers.   They had represented to him the
folly of bringing Europeans into action before
the heats of the day had subsided, together
with the facility evening might give to
their retreat, should they chance to be discomfited; and he would most certainly have
postponed the action till the afternoon, when
an unexpected counsellor demanded to be admitted.

Montoyo had despatched a messenger for Don
Francisco de Aldana, of the Spanish contingent,
an officer who was much esteemed by Sebas-

tian for his gallantry in the field, which was only equalled by his imprudence in the council. Christovao hastened to inform him that the King was about to sacrifice the glorious career of conquest that was before the army of the Cross, by listening to the suggestions of his generals; and the reckless soldier, scarcely waiting to be announced, rushed into the royal presence. Sebastian found an immediate supporter in his former resolves: Aldana declared that already had the enemy cause to tax them with cowardice. "Was the Christian army afraid of the Moors? Did Sebastian of Portugal dread Muley Moloch?" Like a war-cry did these expressions act on the King, and the word was given for the troops to advance.

Return we to the Moorish camp. Slowly the Mahommedan forces took up their position in the plains of Alcazarquiver. Eighty-seven thousand men, disposed in the form of a crescent, at length showed their tremendous front to the gallant and devoted Christians, who mustered little more than fifteen thousand strong. Ten thousand spears rose over the turbaned heads of the Moorish cavalry, forming the points of this vast army, while a cloud of mounted lancemen and musketeers thickening toward the centre, supported the rear, stretching from flank to flank. In the van of the whole were the Andalusian Moors,—who burned to avenge on the Christians the treasured hate of days gone by, — in the second line were the renegades, and the remaining ranks consisted of native infantry, warriors of Fez and Morocco: even the archers of Mount Atlas were there, that the feathered messengers of destruction might share in the work of death, with the leaden ball of the renegade musketeers, the iron bolts of the Arquebusiers, and the deadly fire of forty pieces of artillery. The infantry of Sebastian's army was formed into three lines. The cavalry occupied the centre, and supported the flanks. On the left was the royal standard, surrounded by a sacred band of devoted defenders from among the youthful cavaliers; while the artillery advanced on the right so as to have the full range of the enemy's front, at the same time the little park being kept together, the guns would be more easily protected.

Five times out-numbered by their Mahommedan foes, the gallant Christians quailed not. The battle opened by a general charge of Moorish artillery, which was answered by the cannon of the Portuguese. On came the warriors of the Cross, while that vast crescent seemed to open its ponderous jaws to receive them. The charge of the Christians was for the moment successful. The centre of the Mahommedans wavered and fell into confusion. It was in the rear of this part of his army that the dying Muley Moloch had stationed himself. Yes! the last sand of the Moorish hero was fast running. He had seen the ranks of his army

broken, from the litter in which he reclined:
mingling with his immediate attendants, Beatrice and Zuma beheld the death dews on
his brow, even while he called on the routed
Moors to remember the glory of their sires—
to turn again on the enemy—to crush the
invaders of their native land.

Latava at this moment rode up to the Harife,
and communicated to him that the flanks of
the Mahommedan army were moving to the
assistance of the centre; thus ere long the
Christians must be surrounded.

"My horse, Latava! my horse!"—gasped
the dying Monarch. "Let me join once more
in glorious warfare—let me rally those stricken
cowards — we must conquer— our cause is just
—Allah fights for the crescent!"

Muley Moloch was assisted on his war horse
—his scimitar was again in his hand. At the
sight of their revered Sovereign the tide of fugitives, which had been driven back by the
first charge of the Christians, turned. The

Moors swept past him, calling on Allah to bless the Harife as they rushed to the fight. Latava, Beatrice, and Zuma were, for a moment, the sole companions of Muley Moloch, so enthusiastic had been the effect of this personal appeal to the attachment of his army. The dying hero had scarcely advanced from the spot where he had first mounted, and now he motioned to the Renegade that he would resume his position in the curtained couch that had borne him to the field — the scimitar dropped from his hand — he fell into the arms of Latava, and faltering to the litter, gradually reclined himself on its cushions. Muley Moloch spoke not — his voice had gone forth never again to return till the King should answer for his stewardship of the talents allotted him, before the King of Kings. His head turned slowly round—his leaden gaze was fixed for an instant on the renewed fight — he heard the cry of " Allah Hu !" rise above the faint war-shout of the Christians, as in their turn they had been driven back; and Muley Moloch, placing his finger on his lips, expired.

So significant had been this gesture of the dying Monarch, that the renegade needed not the suggestions of his own prudence to induce him to draw the curtains of the litter. Again it was raised on the shoulders of the bearers, and Muley Moloch was declared to have recovered from a swoon. The standard of the crescent moved before the corse of the hero, and taking up a position on a slight elevation, Latava from time to time appeared to hold communication with his royal master, though in reality himself directing the operations of the Mahommedan army. The Marquis de Montoyo was on that plain the evil genius of his country, guiding the fortunes of the fight. He seemed to have possessed himself of ubiquity. Now he was leading a body of musketeers against a phalanx of Moorish spearmen — " Portugal and the Holy Cross !"—they drive the Mussulmans before them —" What! has Christovao

forgotten this day he fights for the crescent?
Allah Hu! Allah Hu!" A cloud of horse
wheel round yon clump of palms—'twas but a
feint — the Lusitanian ranks are broken — the
Arabs are amongst them — the glistening scimitar drinks the blood of the invaders.

" Back, soldiers, back ! hear ye not the word
of your captain?" It was Montoyo's voice,
calling to a gallant band which had cut its
way, even to the litter of Muley Moloch. In
another moment the corse of the departed
hero would have been in the power of his enemies ;—the head cut off, exposed on a spear,
and the battle lost ; so general would have been
the consternation spread through the Moorish
ranks at the fall of their leader. Sebastian
must have triumphed ; but, no,—the Marquis
de Montoyo had seen the position of the bel-
ligerents at a glance, from a distant part of
the field. The threatened casualty appeared
to him of vital importance to the consummation of his treason. He knew not of Muley

Moloch's death, and dreaded that the Moorish Monarch might be taken prisoner.

Galled by the artillery, which played incessantly on the Christians from the same commanding position on which the litter had been placed by Latava, Sebastian had determined on making a dash at the guns. Gathering round him the élite of his nobility, and joining a squadron of cavalry commanded by Don Pedro Lopas, the whole body of horsemen had charged up the slight acclivity before them, bearing on the musketeers, a battalion of which flanked the artillery. For the second time that day had fortune seemed inclined to favour the Christians. The cannon poured forth one deadly round, and many a trooper bit the dust, but on had come the thundering charge of cavalry. The musketeers could not stand the shock, they fell back in confusion, and the guns of the Mahommedans were for a moment in the power of Sebastian.

" See !" cried the warrior Monarch, who in bright green armour and waving plume had led the onset. " 'Tis Muley Moloch's banner, 'tis the litter of the false Emperor ;—on, Dons and Cavaliers, — Sebastian, Sebastian, — the Holy Cross for Portugal !"

The litter was but at a short distance from the cannon which had just been taken. Before it was the Moorish standard ; and several small banners which had once pointed the corners of Muley Moloch's pavilion, now waved around the corse of the hero.

" The litter ! the litter !—take the usurper alive." Thus shouted Sebastian, as he cut his way through the opposing musketeers. They fell before the power of his arm, which seemed to be possessed of more than human strength. It was at this moment, with head-long speed, Montoyo reached the till then successful Christians. Galloping up to the bewildered Lopas,—who, by Sebastian's impetuosity bereft of command, had been left considerably in the rear of his squadron,—the traitor exclaimed, " Sound the recall, or the King is lost.—The Arab's hordes bear on us."

The retreat sounded, and the obedient soldiers turned.   The Moors rallied;—the musketeers, under the command of Latava, poured a deadly fire on the devoted Portuguese.   The guns were retaken, and again they opened their blazing throats.   Then was it that the gallant De Sá, hearing the order to retreat, said his horse knew not that evolution: rushing on the enemy, he cut his way into their ranks and fell.

Though the cry of Christovao, passing on the command of the deceived Lopas, reached the ear of the exasperated Sebastian as he was borne back by the retreating cavalry, yet he knew not that a traitor spoke; and only cursed the misconception of the Marquis, which had led him to believe the enemy would surround them.   At this period of the action, Latava's musketeers made a rapid movement to follow up the broken squadron. Two fresh battalions from the reserve now supported them, and the rout which had commenced with the discomfiture of Sebastian's last charge, threatened to become general.

A chance shot slightly wounded the barb on which Zuma rode; it started, wheeled round on its haunches, and taking the bit in its teeth, tore along the plain, passing the ranks of the Moorish reserve, and carrying its rider far away from the scene of battle. Willingly would Beatrice have followed her friend, but she was suddenly surrounded by strange soldiers. Too alarmed to discover if they were friends or foes, she momentarily expected death: but a danger, to which death had been mercy, was near her. Had she even fallen into the hands of Christovao, she could only have been sacrificed to his burst of passion, or failing to obtain communication with Sebastian, be returned to the living death from which she had escaped in the Casa de Pena; but the danger that threatened her arose not from her brother. Whatever had been his intentions respecting her, his whole soul was now occupied in the execution of his treachery toward Sebastian : he knew not even that Beatrice was almost within his grasp. It was from the execution of Latava's preconcerted scheme, that arose the immediate peril of the Donna. By the death of Muley Moloch the Genoese saw, as he imagined, the only obstacle to his securing possession of the fair Portuguese removed; he had therefore despatched a messenger to countermand his previous orders given to a small band of renegades, whom he had directed to keep in a compact body, as much as possible avoid actual encounter with the enemy, and, at the first favourable opportunity, seize the Donna and bear her to a place of security in the city of Alcazarquiver. In the early part of the day Latava had found it necessary,—on perceiving the change of costume between the Christian hostages,—to send a communication by the same trusty follower, for the direction of his emissaries. His first mission effected, the messenger had returned to his master; but in his second attempt to reach his comrades he had been slain; and the original orders of Latava were consequently carried into effect.

When the Renegade had driven back the sudden attack of Sebastian's devoted band, and returned, in pursuance of the deceit he continued to practise, for the purpose of apparently communicating with Muley Moloch, Beatrice had disappeared. He at first imagined that she had been borne off by the Christians; but in this he was immediately undeceived, as one of his soldiers remained to inform him that his orders had been punctually executed.

" It is better even as it has occurred," thought Latava. " The Christians cannot contend with us much longer. It is but to fetch my fair captive from the town, and this night shall she be mine, whether the scene of my triumph be in the city or the camp."

Return we to Sebastian. He had fallen back on his own artillery, his chosen cavalry hardly pressed by the Moors. Again he charged — and the Infidels for a moment received a check. It was then that two, the last of five brothers who had together entered the field among the most daring of Sebastian's Portuguese, were seen standing on a mound of slain, holding fast and battling for a standard they had jointly taken from the enemy. One of these was Nicolao. — On his return from Portugal he had come up with the army at the commencement of the action; and he had for the first time neared his royal master, when he beheld his brother combating for a Mahommedan standard. Together they won the proud trophy of their valour: but they were surrounded, — nobly they fought and fell. The bravest of the Christians had fallen by these repeated charges; while the Mahommedans, reinforced by fresh troops, retired but to return with redoubled strength.

Wherever the battle raged with the greatest fury, there was Sebastian. Twice was he wounded,—twice was he dashed to the earth, —his horse being shot under him. When his first charger was killed, and Dom George de Albuquerque, anxious to remount him, essayed to take the fallen monarch from his saddle, coagulated blood was found to have glued him to his seat. Nor was the bold example of their King lost on that army of heroes. Dom Duarte de Menezes was slain, with the whole of his veteran followers from Tangiers. By the last charge of Sebastian the chief of the Christian cavaliers fell: to enumerate them by name belongs not to our narrative. Even Dom Sebastian, when he looked on his routed forces, despaired; for that which had been a well-contested battle, was now a slaughter of almost defenceless men.   Lifting on high his blood-stained sword, a moment he gazed upward, as if commending his soul to Heaven; he then looked blandly around,—but few familiar faces met his eye;—and pointing to an advancing body of Moors, the desperate monarch dashed headlong into the midst of the fight.

The Portuguese infantry attempted to rally. They were broken by the Moorish horse, and fled in complete disorder.   The Castilians fell to a man, and proved themselves the bravest troops on the field.   The Germans and other auxiliaries behaved with great gallantry, selling their lives dearly; and the bold Stukely found in the plains of Alcazarquiver his last fight.— Sebastian had disappeared.

The rout now became general.   The army of the Christians was delivered over as a prey to the destroyer.   Quarter was neither asked nor given, and till the sun set on that red field the sword ceased not to slay.   Night brought the jackal, the tiger-cat, and the leopard, to glut on the slain. The dogs of the city found that a stronger than they were in possession of the feast, whilst the vulture could but tear a fragment of reeking flesh, and bear it away from the wild beasts of the plain.

When Zadig and Abdallah found, on their arrival at the Moorish camp, that the armies had engaged, and learned, by inquiry, that the Senhoras had gone forth with the Mahommedan hosts, they repaired with all despatch to the plains of Alcazarquiver. As they approached the field, Zadig regarded the conflict with intense interest; but not so Abdallah, who gravely moralized on the scene before them, and though not appalled by their proximity to danger, told his nephew that, but for his oath's sake, he would have sought some other opportunity of offering service to the Donna Beatrice, rather than look on to behold man wantonly destroy his fellow. They had reached a part of the field which gave them a view of the rising ground, where Sebastian had so nearly made himself master of the litter containing the corse of Muley Moloch. It was just after this desperate charge that Zadig, standing in his stirrups, and gazing around in the hope of discovering the position wherein it was most likely the Senhoras had been bestowed, caught sight of a page in grey and black, attempting to restrain a horse, which with furious speed was skirting the fight. It was Zuma, whose barb fast bearing her away from the battle, appeared, to the eye of Zadig, the Donna Beatrice.

"Abdallah—brother of my father—remember thine oath !—follow me !" exclaimed the young Moor, and in another moment he tore along the plain. Abdallah at a more moderate pace pursued in the rear of his reckless kinsman; but ere either of them could come up with the object of their pursuit, a sudden movement in the belligerent parties involved both in the confusion of the fight. Zadig exchanged blows with Moors or Christians — it mattered not to him ; they all seemed leagued against his following the supposed Beatrice—till he was unhorsed by the fall of his jaded steed, and long was it ere he disengaged himself from the mêlée that surrounded him. Abdallah, on losing sight of Zadig, continued in search of him, till falling in with a party of Bedouins, plundering the dead and dying, as the tide of battle ebbed and flowed, he zealously employed himself in the hard task of endeavouring to prevent the more cruel excesses of these desperate marauders. In his sacred character, as a marabout, his power over them was great. Though the Berébers as a people,—considering themselves the aborigines of the soil,—despised both Arab and Moor, Abdallah from his long wanderings had become familiar with the children of the desert, and obtained a sway among them which he generally exercised as a man of peace.

CHAPTER XXII.

THE TWO MONARCHS.

THE swelling tide of the M'Hazen had borne
its ensanguined waves past the field of fight,
and many a corse of man and steed were hurried along by its waters, escaping sword and
shot, but finding death in the angry ford. The
hapless Muley Hamet,—he who had invited the
invader to the land which would not that he
should reign over it,—had there perished. The
bodies of the dead had swept down the stream ;
—the noise of the battle had subsided into the
distant shout of the pursuit, when Sebastian, a
solitary fugitive, approached the river. By a
seeming miracle he had survived the battle,—

extricated himself from the flight of his army, and with feeble steps had sought the stream to drink.   How bitter is the thirst of the wounded man, he who has heard the cry of "water! water!" from wretches whose blood is counting by each welling drop the moments of existence, need not be told,—and others of our readers we have sufficiently initiated in the horrors of war.

The Marquis de Montoyo had indeed triumphed.   Reckless and imprudent had been the expedition; but fortune, as we have shown, in more than one instance, seemed about to declare for Sebastian, when Christovao,—this secret avenger of imagined wrongs,—this blind betrayer of that monarch who, had he conquered, would ere long have proclaimed his alliance with the house of Montoyo,—changed the fortune of the day, working his own ruin with the destruction of his royal master.

When Sebastian cut his way amid the ranks of the enemy, which closing around him hid the King from the anxious sight of his devoted followers, Christovao beheld the desperate act of the royal warrior, and for the moment shared in the belief which in Portugal remained undisputed for many years, that Sebastian survived not the unequal fight :—but the event had been otherwise ordained. So great was the dread his power had created amongst the enemy, that each arm of that opposing host was only stretched out as a shield and a defence against one whom the Mahommedans imagined more than human. Thus the King, who was, in point of fact, seeking death in the midst of his foes, actually made good his retreat, with but a single additional wound to those he had already received.

Leaving Sebastian stretched on the banks of the M'Hazen, we will follow Montoyo, who, assuming the distinctive badge of Muley Moloch's army, had sought Latava for the purpose of demanding his hostages of the Emperor, whom he still imagined in existence. He found that the Renegade, immediately the battle was decided, had returned to the Mahommedan camp, and repairing thither, was admitted to his tent. The hostages were not to be recovered: the Genoese honestly denying all knowledge of the fate which might have attended Zuma, while, with respect to Beatrice, he appeared to be equally uninformed, though when Christovao joined him he was about to proceed to the city of Alcazarquiver, for the purpose of conducting his fair prize to the encampment. Here he had more than sufficient sway to hold her in possession, he having just received the promise of high office from the new Sovereign of Fez and Morocco, who was known among Europeans as Muley Mahomet the bastard.

"And am I thus to be cheated after all I have done for the Moorish cause?" demanded Montoyo. "I insist on an interview with Muley Moloch."

"Thou shalt have it," replied Latava calmly, for the anticipated consummation of his desires enabled him to control his rising ire. "Follow me."

The Marquis instantly obeyed his bidding, too proud to hold further conference with the Renegade, whose interference with the Emperor he inwardly cursed himself for having solicited, and he now nerved himself to demand at once the hostages of his treason. The Genoese turned ever and anon to look at his companion, as if in thorough wantonness of spirit dallying with Christovao's evident anxiety to possess himself of the objects of his love and hate, for such his unguarded expressions had declared them to be. The crowd which was assembled around the pavilion of Muley Moloch made way for Latava and Montoyo. The curtains were withdrawn by attendant Moors, and instantly closed on the multitude.

"Now make thine appeal," tauntingly exclaimed the Renegade.

The corse of Muley Moloch was stretched on a bier raised about three feet from the floor of the tent. His attenuated form was robed as in life. The costly tunic, the jewelled belt, and

flowing trowsers, he had worn in the field of
battle, had not yet been removed. His turban,
bearing on its front a diamond of great price,
and wreathed with strings of the fairest pearls,
mocked the livid face of the dead with the bau-
bles of life. One single fold alone of the many
twined with these costly gems gave decency to
that silent image of the departed, in supporting
the lower jaw, and the pale thin lips were com-
pressed as when in mute eloquence the finger of
the hero had rested there. The long dark
beard lay on the gold-wrought vest of the monarch, giving a grave majesty to the composed
features ; and his right hand was placed on the
scimitar which had fallen from his grasp when
the hand refused its office in death. Six eunuchs stood beside the bier, and candelabra
burning aromatic oils shed a fragrance through
the pavilion ; while at the lower end, gazing on
that quiet face, were two old Moors resting on
the long spears with which they guarded the
dead, whom nought could harm.

Such was the scene which was presented to
the view of the Marquis de Montoyo as he entered the tent of Muley Moloch. For the moment his surprise had kept him silent, but soon
his anger at being thus trifled with, sought vent
in terms of uncontrolled rage. He found himself addressing a soldier, who had taken the
place of the Renegade by his side, his conduc-
tor having left the pavilion. Christovao, infuriated by the supercilious treatment he had
received, rushed past the Moor in pursuit of
Latava ; but he was met at the entrance of the
tent by a strong guard, who immediately securing him, convinced the impetuous Montoyo
that his intention had been provided against.
Conducted to the extremity of the camp, his
horse was given up to him, and he was permitted to depart, but communication with the new
Harife was, by Latava's direction, denied ; and
Christovao found the first fruits of his treason
in neglect and insult from those whose favour
and protection he imagined purchased by his

services. Almost maddened by this reflection, he turned his horse in the direction of the fatal field of Alcazarquiver, in the latent hope that it might really be as Latava had informed him; and Zuma and Beatrice, having disappeared during the fight, he should still by some fortunate chance recover them among the fugitives.

CHAPTER XXIII.

THE MOORISH GIRL.

Christovao de Montoyo, on approaching the field of battle, perceived that even the pursuit had ended: all the Christians who had not made good their retreat, being either prisoners or slain. Piquets of the Mahommedan army occasionally passed him on their route to and from the camp, to whom he had again and again to show the safe conduct of the late Emperor: the sun had sunk beneath the horizon, and Christovao directed his course towards the town in search of an abode for the night, resolving on the morrow to make his services known to Muley Mahomet, the now acknowledged Harife, claiming his protection and assistance in tracing Zuma and Beatrice. He had thrown the reins carelessly on the neck of his horse, and was proceeding at a pace as agreeable to the jaded animal as it was to his own worn frame and unstrung nerves ; when in the distance he beheld a wounded cavalier, his head uncovered, his armour unclasped and broken, making his way over a hillock of palms hiding a little dell beside the river from the road Montoyo was pursuing. The eye of hate is as quick as the glance of love, and the Marquis recognized Sebastian.

" Now will I make him my prisoner, ransom or no ransom. If Christovao must turn renegade, this royal seducer shall be his slave,—he is in my power—his life is in my hands—now will I taunt him—now tell this abject King the dishonour done to the house of Montoyo hath worked his fall."

Like a stream of mental fire, awaking the dormant faculties of Christovao, these thoughts rapidly passed through his mind. He checked his horse, and watched the fugitive slowly descend towards the river. The traitor felt certain of his prey. He again moved gently forward : arriving at the stump of a tree, some distance from the bank over which Sebastian had disappeared, he secured the reins of his horse, and feeling that his arms were ready for use, with cautious step advanced on foot. A priest in the garments of his holy office, seemed hastening in the same direction, but Christovao regarded him not ; he had reached a thicket of aloes, from whence he beheld, as in a small amphitheatre surrounded by the rising ground, a sight which awoke the wildest rage in his ungovernable spirit.

Sebastian was lying on the earth supported in the arms of a page, whose costume was the same which had attracted his attention in the pavilion of Muley Moloch, and which he naturally assigned to Beatrice. The head of the wounded King was bare, and the blood flowed from a long gash across the forehead, which his companion was attempting to staunch by the application of a bandage steeped in water. It was Zuma who ministered to the hapless monarch : far away from the battle had she been carried by her horse, which throwing its rider, left her several miles from the scene of action. Slowly returning along the river, in search of Beatrice, she was already in the little dell when Sebastian descended ; but ere he recognized her, the wounded man had fainted from exhaustion, and she now attempted his restoration to consciousness,—a task that seemed past her skill, so great had been his loss of blood. Her head was bowed towards the face of the King, and Montoyo imagined he beheld his sister supporting in her arms the paramour who had dishonoured her. Bursting through the thicket with a bound which brought him within a pace of the Moorish girl, in another instant Christovao had passed his stiletto into the heart of Zuma.

" Die, Beatrice De Montoyo !" shouted the

infuriated man. " Thus let the mingling of thy blood with thy seducer's wash out the stain of our dishonour."

" Forbear ! forbear !" Rising above the eminence which the Marquis had just descended, Christovao beheld in priestly robes a form he had long since imagined to have departed from the earth. It was the ancient Marquis de Montoyo. " Forbear ! Slay not the youth, touch not the sacred person of Sebastian, thy liege King. What !" continued the old man, " is it Christovao with the Moorish scarf ? Then is thy treason declared, and thou dost glory in it. Oh ! cursed, cursed deed."

With arms uplifted as if in malediction, the patriarch approached his son ; but Christovao's treachery was already punished. Zuma had died without a groan, and as her face turned towards her slayer, had the shade of his father seemed to rise from the earth and proclaim his treason. He saw those fond eyes, which even the pangs of death robbed not of

their lustre, fixed on him. What cared he now
that the tomb had opened its marble jaws to
give forth an accusing spirit ? — what cared he
now that his enemy lay weltering in his gore ?
—what cared he now for dread of Hell or hope
of Heaven ?

"Curse on, old man, curse on!" cried
Christovao, dashing his casque from his head,
and twining his fingers in his hair as he tore it
from his temples ; "See! there—there ! I have
slain the only being I ever loved."

He had fallen to the earth as if death-
stricken, and his father bent over him almost
in the hope that life had departed from one who
must live dishonoured. The deep breathing of
the wretched man convinced the old Marquis
that his son was yet alive, and an object of
paramount importance called for his attention.
Carefully examining the wounds of Sebastian,
he applied a styptic which staunched the blood ;
and after having bandaged them, producing a
cordial from the folds of his robe, he poured a

small quantity into the mouth of the wounded monarch, whose face he continued bathing till it exhibited signs of approaching animation.

" Christovao," said the old man with a tone of authority, " go forth from the presence of thy King ;— he revives, and must not see a traitor."

" By Heaven he dies !—'tis he who caused this ruin !" exclaimed Christovao, starting on his feet, and feeling for the stiletto which had already done enough of evil. It had fallen by the body of its victim, and as his eye turned towards the corse of the Moorish girl, he was again unmanned, and throwing himself on the body franticly embraced it. The aged Montoyo had continued seated by Sebastian, stedfastly regarding his son, who had neither in word or deed recognized him.

" Dost thou not know me ?" asked the old man. " Thou didst think me dead—behold, I am alive !"

" I see thou art by some strange providence

restored to life," slowly replied Christovao, raising his head from the earth; " and ministering to one, who, to thy daughter's shame, hath foully wrought dishonour on our house."

" Hold, hold!" interrupted the old man. " Shame never rested on our ancient name till thou didst become traitor. Beatrice hath hidden from thee that which it were well she had revealed. Unhappy mystery, which seems to hang a pall above the fortunes of our race! He who doth secretly avenge, must wrong his enemy though his cause be just. Thou hast thy recompence. Hadst thou confronted Dom Sebastian—he who is now here, stricken nigh unto death,—he would have told thee what I tell thee now—thy sister is a lawful wife. She would have been a Queen, but thou didst rob her husband of a kingdom. Pray Heaven thy treason doth not touch his life ;" and here the Marquis de Montoyo, for so we must now call him, again busied himself in the recovery of the wounded King.

" It is strange, most strange !" said Christovao in musing distraction, his hands clasped
before him, as seated on the ground he gazed
about him with a bewildered expression of
countenance which seemed to threaten the approach of insanity.

" Hath, then, Sebastian wedded Beatrice?—
The hope I cherished been realized, and now
by me destroyed ? And Zuma, Zuma, whose
heart was mine,—who patiently would bear
with me in angry word or deed,—nor thwarted
me in aught, except to stay my fatal, blind
revenge on Beatrice,—my hand hath slain,
seeking a sister's life. Oh, father, father ! wherefore didst thou leave thy son to wrestle with
these mysteries ? How art thou yet alive? and
living, wherefore didst thou not stay my wayward course ? I sought but to avenge the
honour of our house."

" But Zuma," replied the old man reproachfully —" was it to the honour of that
house thou didst betray her ? Behold, the

King revives! 'Tis well he knows thee not, with yonder Moorish badge — give me thy horse. Unhappy wretch! thy treason will protect thee — honest men must flee before the rising moon invites the infidels to prowl abroad in search of captives mid the wounded."

The Marquis waited not his son's reply, for Christovao was again lost in deep thought ;— his dilated eyes fixed on the face of the corse before him. Supporting Sebastian, whose limbs had partially regained their office, though he continued mentally unconscious, the old man assisted him to mount the horse which had been quietly grazing on the fresh herbage near the river. Waving his hand to Christovao, he exclaimed, " Farewell — I leave thee with the ruin thou hast wrought — I will not curse thee—no! Forsake thy sins, eschew ambition, flee this land of infidels, and I will pray of Heaven to pardon thee."

Thus saying, the old Montoyo carefully

mounted behind the King, who was unable to remain in an upright position. He allowed the royal
sufferer to recline on his breast, and putting
the horse to a fast walk, they departed in the
direction of the ford, which the Marquis hoped
they might be able to cross, so as to join the
principal portion of the fugitives belonging to
the army who had taken that route. Con-
tinuing on the banks of the river, he was ere
long alarmed by the appearance of a small
body of horsemen galloping toward them. To
fly was impossible, for the animal they be-
strode already began to show symptoms of
distress, at a double burthen concluding the
fatigues of that toilsome day both to horse and
man. On came the strangers, and the Marquis drew his bridle in the faint hope that they
might prove friends who had missed the ford,
as the pursuit of the discomfited Portuguese
had long terminated, the Moors being content
with the decisive victory they had gained.

The moon was fast rising, and the aged Montoyo trembled with agitation as he strained his powers of vision to detect the character of the approaching party : at length, discerning them to be Arabs, all hope forsook him. He thought not of himself : it mattered little to one whose days were hastening to a close,—whose peace was made with Heaven,—who felt that he had already lived too long in beholding the treason of his son,—that the end of his pilgrimage seemed now at hand, or in captivity would speedily arrive. No! in that moment of peril he thought but of his King — that Sebastian, falling into the power of his enemies, should die unprepared and unshriven, or be made the instrument of the infidels in regaining possession of the Portuguese garrisons in Africa,— their certain course of proceeding when demanding his ransom,—oppressed the Marquis, not as the sudden idea of a moment, but as the consummation of his worst fears since his discovery of the wounded monarch. Unwilling as we are to leave the ancient Montoyo in this strait, it is necessary, for the clearer conduct of our story, that we accompany Latava to Alcazarquiver.

CHAPTER XXIV.

A REUNION.

Latava, fully intending that his passion for Beatrice should not interfere with his political views,—and being well aware how necessary it was for him to continue in close attendance on the new Harife so long as it was the royal pleasure to keep the field,—had determined on removing his fair captive to the camp on the evening after the battle. To secure himself against surprise from the Bedouin marauders, who were abroad, he had with him a guard of some six trusty lances, all Genoese, devoted to their commander. Pricking forward across the plains, they were not long in reaching

Alcazarquiver; and, leaving his followers at one of the principal entrances of the city, Latava hastened to the habitation where, by his order, Beatrice had been placed in durance.

That morning the unhappy Donna had been suddenly surrounded by an armed party, who appeared unconnected with the fight, and determined on her capture. Ere she could resist or flee, her bridle was seized; her horse was guided through the intricacies of the fight; and, to her astonishment and alarm, she perceived that she was a prisoner. However distressed Beatrice might have been in the Moorish camp by the uncontrolled expression of Latava's libertine gaze, the Renegade had never dared to express his passion in words, and the thought that his emissaries were her captors did not occur to her. The features of the turbaned soldiers were not Moorish, and she considered them, for the moment, disguised followers of her brother. Her screams were unattended to amid the roar of the conflict.—

Afar off, she beheld the plume of her royal husband waving, surrounded by combatants :—the instant before her capture, she was praying to the saints for safety in that hour of peril; and, if a miracle could have been wrought in her behalf, gladly would she have found herself once more in the Casa de Pena;—but now, as she was rapidly borne along the plain by her silent conductors,—torn, as she imagined, for ever from Sebastian, to rejoin whom she had risked so much, she franticly exclaimed,

" Take me back to the battle,—the King will reward you;—place me only within the protection of his arm; I ask no more.   My brother has no claim upon me; believe me, he has not !"

" Is she mad ?" said a Genoese, who seemed to command the party, as Beatrice, failing in her entreaties, attempted to throw herself from her horse. " Get thee up behind her, and hold this termagant masquerader," continued he to one of his soldiers: " but use her gently, as thou wilt be answerable to Latava."

Beatrice understood little of this communication between the renegades, except the mention of Latava; but in that name her fate seemed disclosed. Stunned by the extent of her misery, and almost fainting in the arms of the trooper who supported her, she had been conducted to Alcazarquiver: the Donna was therefore perfectly prepared for a visit from the Renegade, who, unannounced, entered the apartment which had been made her prison.

" The beautiful Beatrice de Montoyo has, I hope, forgiven the restraint which has been placed on her," said Latava, taking the hand of the weeping girl.

" I will forgive, forget all, if thou wilt restore me even to my brother: but oh ! if chivalry is not dead in thee, tell me how fares the gallant King of Portugal ?—How speeds the fight ?"

" Gently, fair Donna," replied the Renegade ;
" thou askest too many questions.   It is not of
war and war's alarms I came to speak, but of
love and love's soft dalliance : nor have I time
for even this, until we reach the camp :—thus
much thy taste for warlike enterprise shall be
indulged, fair page ;"—and Latava passed his
arm round Beatrice, attempting to draw her
towards him.

" Release me !" exclaimed the frantic girl :
" I am no romantic maiden, love-lorn and following her lover to the wars ;—though, the holy
Mother of Heaven knows, love-lorn I am indeed.—Latava !"—she sank on her knees to the
relentless Renegade—" I am a wife ! Now thou
wilt protect me, I know thou wilt : tell me
how speeds the fight;—I cannot longer hold
disguise ;—does Sebastian live ?—is he a con-
queror ?"

" Disguise ! most noble maiden, or wife,
or page, or whatsoever thou pleasest to be
called," responded the Renegade, on whom the

distress of Beatrice made no impression, except as it delayed their getting to the gates ere they would be closed for the night, " thou shalt have robes of cloth of gold, and wondrous specimens of curious needlework, in place of these boy's trappings. But this is no time for converse; many a captive to-day have I lost in thinking only of thee. Thy King, thy countrymen, are slain or fugitives; and thou art mine by all the usages of war.".

He seized the shrinking girl, and lifting her in his arms, bore her along the hall of the dwelling.

" Oh ! if I am at thy mercy, 'tis well Sebastian died !" exclaimed Beatrice; and loudly she shrieked for help.

So, then, thou art the fair mistress of this moral king, after all thy marriage claims : but thou hast tongue enough for any wife in Europe," said Latava, as he passed a scarf across the mouth of his captive to stop her cries. Beatrice struggled in vain; she was lifted on her horse by the servile owner of the abode where she had been detained, who was a creature of Latava's, and in a few moments had passed the gates of the town.

" Thou hast added to our number, Rinaldo," remarked the Renegade to the officer of his little guard, on perceiving that, instead of six followers, nine were in his train.

" Three stragglers from Ben Hadad's Moorish lances, my lord, whose horses knocked up during the pursuit :—they have been refreshing in the town, and now bear us company to the camp."

" 'Tis well; I suppose thou knowest them ?" rejoined Latava.

" I do, my captain, or they should not make fellowship with us. Kaled and two of his brother troopers are the men."

" Then let them push forward as our advanced guard, and look well that we fall not into a Bedouin ambush : those robbers care not to fight till after the battle; they will strike you twenty blows for plunder, while they cannot afford one for honest warfare."

Three horsemen passed him as the order was obeyed; and among them was the Turk whose shoulder still bore the bruise of Latava's pistol, but the Renegade remembered him not. Ever ready to strike, visiting on others his fury when out of temper with himself, he took little account where his blows fell: but Kaled, being a sufferer, had not so short a memory.

"Thou wouldst like more air, perhaps?" said the Genoese to his captive, whom he supported before him on his powerful charger.

"Oh that I might die!" exclaimed Beatrice, thus using the licence which a removal of the scarf allowed her.

"Nay, that were ungrateful, after all the trouble I have taken in thy behalf," laughingly remarked the Renegade. He received no answer to his taunt but sobs. "Thou dost shame thy manly attire, page! Cheer thee, cheer thee; thou shalt reign queen of my harem."

As Latava made this gallant concession to the distress of Beatrice,—albeit for many a long year unused to soothe even a woman's woes,—the three horsemen in the advance suddenly wheeled off to the right, and a small party of mounted Arabs, emerging from a hollow in the road, charged the renegades. Latava, encumbered by his captive, was for the moment inactive; but Beatrice soon relieved him of this embarrassment. Disengaging herself from his grasp, and sliding from the horse, she gained the cover which the assailants had just quitted, and hid herself amid some acacia bushes to await the event of this unexpected affray. It was soon decided. The attacking party more than twice outnumbered the attacked: Latava for a while supported the unequal fight; —one antagonist he had already slain, and was engaged with a second combatant, whom, though an excellent swordsman, the superior strength and skill of the Renegade promised soon to overcome; when Kaled,—till now only a witness of the fight, though his companions were active sharers in it,—suddenly pushed towards the Genoese.

' "Blood for the blow!" shouted the Mahomedan, and his scimitar was plunged to the hilt.

Thus died Latava the Renegade.

"Thou didst not use him fairly," remarked an aged Beréber as he sternly regarded his late antagonist.

" Methinks a soldier may avenge himself how he can when an Augur takes to the sword ; — I told thee but an hour ago I owed him deadly hate, and I have paid him in his death."

" I fought, as I imagined, for a maiden of our tribe, for the daughter of my brother : from what thou saidst I supposed her in captivity, but find now mine error. It was the fair Christian girl Latava would have carried to the camp; she has hidden herself in yonder hollow." Abdallah, for it was the Marabout,

lifted up his eyes to Heaven : " Allah is just !
I swore to protect this maiden, and, even when
I knew it not, have I rescued her."

The voice of the old Arab calling her name
was soon answered by Beatrice, who felt indeed
grateful for this providential deliverance. On the
fall of their leader the renegades had fled, leaving several of their comrades slain on the field.
Kaled remained with the victors; his two companions were Bedouins of the tribe to which
Abdallah had for the time attached himself. The Moor, resolved on avenging the
blow he had received from Latava, happened
to have remarked Beatrice borne from the field
of battle in the direction of Alcazarquiver by
a party of Genoese lancers. He had moreover
heard from the soldier who had been left to acquaint their captain with the fulfilment of his
orders, what appeared to the man Latava's incomprehensible dissatisfaction at the execution
of his own directions ; and all this awoke in
Kaled a curiosity to know what might be

his real intention with respect to one of the hostages so much favoured by Muley Moloch; their sex being generally known. Whatever he might discover he felt assured could be used to the injury of the Renegade; or why so much secrecy in the affair? Under this impression he had followed Latava to the camp, and from thence, at a sufficient distance to be secure from observation, on his route to Alcazarquiver. It was on the plain that he fell in with Abdallah, who having given up all hope of finding Beatrice, when recognised by Kaled, was proceeding with the Bedouins along the river, on their route to a Dowar they had pitched a few miles on the other side of the M'Hazen.

The Marabout was not unknown to Kaled: thus he immediately claimed acquaintance, to avoid being plundered; and, as a return for the courtesy of his protection from the wild Arabs, he mentioned the capture of the hostage. Abdallah, deceived by the soldier's description, and ignorant of the change of dress which had taken place between the Senhoras, imagined that Zuma was in the hands of Latava. By his authority over the Bedouins he easily engaged them to attempt her rescue; and two of the party, decked in some of the spoils of the day, making them appear like regular Moorish troops, had accompanied Kaled for the purpose of leading the renegades into an ambuscade, should they, as he supposed, intend the removal of their captive to the camp.

The Moor, having slain an officer of Latava's rank, cared not to return to the army, and therefore now joined company with the Arabs. Beatrice, assured by Abdallah that she should speedily be placed under Zadig's protection, was mounted on a horse which had belonged to one of the fallen; and the party, avoiding the ford, then guarded by Moorish troops likely to lighten them of their plunder, was proceeding further up the M'Hazen, where the river, though deep, was not broad, a small islet breaking the distance. Here they would be

able to swim their unladen horses, and trans-
port the heavier spoil by means of a boat
previously concealed to provide against such
a casualty.

Such were the Arabs who approached the
Marquis de Montoyo and the wounded King,
as related in our last chapter. The foremost
horsemen, immediately they perceived the wayfarers, dashed forward to surround them. Montoyo, at the moment imagining immediate death
or captivity certain, offered up a prayer to
Heaven, and awaited the event; but ere a hand
could be laid on them to their injury, Abdallah,
leaving Beatrice, by whose side he had been
riding, had interposed his powerful protection
in behalf of the prisoners.

" My children, they resist not : they are delivered into your hands, and must pay heavy
ransom ; but harm them not !" he exclaimed :
and his followers willingly gave place to the
old man, that he might examine their captives ;
trusting his superior intelligence might ascer-

tain their rank and position in the Christian army, a point on which depended the value of the prize they had made.

" Thou seemest a man of mercy,—dost know this cavalier ?" said Montoyo in the Arabic language, with which he was well acquainted. Abdallah looked with much attention at the King, who, aroused from his lethargy, was now gazing inquiringly around.

" I know him not, but as a suffering fellow-man. This day has my hand been lifted to take life, and I had thought the hour of violence was past with me. Thou must go with us, and pay ransom for thy freedom ; but I will ensure thy life,—blood shall not be shed. Thou hast journeyed along the banks of the M'Hazen; sawest thou a Moorish youth, and a girl dressed as a page in grey and black ? They fled at the end of the fight in the direction thou hast come from."

" The youth I have not seen,—the damsel is slain," said Montoyo solemnly : " would that

I could give thee better intelligence in return for thy protection!"

By this time Beatrice had joined them, in the hope of learning tidings from the strangers ; fearing to hear Latava's report of Sebastian's death confirmed, and yet anxious to know the truth. The voice of the ancient Marquis was a sound familiar to her ear :—where had she last heard those tones ? but—moment of unutterable rapture !—she beheld Sebastian ! , and every other consideration was lost in that blissful recognition. The royal sufferer, though too weak even to breathe her name, became perfectly conscious that Beatrice was by his side, in strange disguise and in a foreign land. It seemed a dream—a fevered fantasy : he held out his arms to her ; she threw herself from her horse, hiding her face in his blood-stained vest. He leant over his beloved, pressing his lips to her pallid cheek ; while again that familiar voice which had before attracted her attention spoke.

" This is no time for greetings: mount, Donna Beatrice ; let us seek the ford."

Without remonstrance she obeyed ; but the direction of the party was changed by the advice of Abdallah, who, for the reasons we have stated, chose another part of the river. Beatrice had now the satisfaction of supporting Sebastian in her arms as they were pushed across the stream, resting on the plunder of the marauders; and here Montoyo, though he would not yet discover himself to his daughter, informed her that Zuma was slain. The circumstances attending her death he disclosed not, in mercy to Beatrice. He allowed her to believe that her friend had fallen by one of the casualties of the fight; but the blow fell heavily on her newly-awakened joy at finding Sebastian yet alive. Once more Montoyo reminded her that the present was no time for the indulgence of her feelings, and she silently acknowledged the appeal. Bitterly her tears flowed for Zuma, the companion of her youth : her husband was wounded, perhaps even unto death ;—but, was he not again restored to her ?

Could she be comfortless? was not this a balm
for all her sufferings?—and with such reflections
she tried to nerve herself against toils and perils
that might still await her.   For that day, however, these were speedily at an end.   A further
ride of about an hour's duration brought the
captives to the Arab Dowar, where they were
insured rest and protection through the influence of Abdallah.

CHAPTER XXV.

A FUNERAL PILE.

The moon had risen high over the little dell where Christovao still sat by the corse of Zuma in utter prostration of spirit. He stirred not, save to part the ringlets from that brow on which death had set its seal; and then, wildly regarding the dim eyes he dared not close, though their fixed, leaden gaze maddened him, he would clasp his hands, and bow his head on his heaving chest, moaning as though in pain. If he had formed any plan beyond watching beside Zuma, to scare the wild beasts from their prey, or tempt them to slay him, it might be he remained there in

the hope of being discovered by some of the
Mahomedan soldiery, and assisted in removing the body of the Moorish girl into the camp;
but the hours crept on, and none had come
save a vulture, who sat on a neighbouring
pine, as if watching till she might claim the
forsaken corse.

" Begone, begone! thou shalt not touch
her!" shouted Christovao, hurling the broken
branch of a tree at the unclean bird.

" Who calls? who calls?" answered a voice:
and Zadig the Moor stood before the slayer of
his sister. The face of Zuma was upturned in
the pale moonlight. The dress deceived not
Zadig, for the brow was dark, and the crimson
stain told the fate of her whom, seeking not, he
had found ;—the Moor having continued his
search for Beatrice till then, nor thought he
of his sister. To find her thus was the greater
pang: and who was watching by her? even
the betrayer of the confiding girl!—he whom
Zadig had sworn should die, or wed her!

Christovao, who had sunk into his former position after scaring the bird away, raised his head as the Moor confronted him.—The brother was pointing to the sister's corse.

"Whose handiwork is this?" he exclaimed in a voice which startled the vulture returning to her seat; and again she rose in the air, and flapped her dusky wing over a scene which promised well that her board should be fully spread.

"I slew her," answered Christovao, calmly regarding Zadig. "Avenge thyself; I am ready, and have no wish to live."

"Thou her murderer!" emphatically demanded the Moor, coming closer to Montoyo till his tall form leant over the destroyer of his sister, who sat unmoved by the corse. "Thou hast dishonoured her, but thou didst love her;—thou couldst not slay!"

Zadig knelt by the side of Zuma, and pressed his lip to her cold cheek, but no tear dimmed the fierceness of his eye. Rising slowly to his full height, he once more confronted Christovao.

"Tell me who worked this deed of blood ?"

"I have said it, Moor : a Montoyo lies not."

"Lies not, false traitor !" shouted Zadig ;—"each Christian curses thee, as he speeds his flight. Lies not ! But I believe thee; 'tis a hellish deed, and thou hast done it."

Thus taunted, the dying embers of Christovao's fiery spirit once again burnt up: he sprang to his feet, and drawing a short sword, rushed towards his maligner, who was not long in meeting Montoyo's weapon with his scimitar. A few moments decided the contest, —Zadig desperately wounded his opponent.

"'Tis well," exclaimed Christovao, sinking to the earth. "I shall now die. Listen to me, Moor. In my blind fury to destroy my sister for a crime she never wrought, I did slay Zuma—Zuma whom I loved ! Dost read the mystery now ?"

" I do," moodily answered Zadig : " the star that guided her whom thou hast killed was ever malignant in its aspect, and violence was in the house of death. Thou hast destroyed a young and beauteous girl, whom living thou didst love, and yet dishonour. There were strange and adverse destinies in this. Well, thou hast judged rightly at the last; thou art worthy of death, and thou shalt die." Here, taking Montoyo's sword from the ground where it had fallen, he poised it in his hand. The wounded man quailed not.

" Strike !" exclaimed Christovao. " I am ready."

" It is not time," answered the Moor. " Dost see yonder planet ? It hovers above the waters of El M'Hazen, as though weighed down by the dense black cloud o'ershadowing the moon. That star is setting. It rose on Zuma's birth :—now, as yon world of light, where death is not, declines, so shall decline thy span of life. Watch thou, and tell me how thy fate rides on."

Thus saying, he deliberately commenced hewing off the branches of a blighted pine-tree. Heavy clouds betokened a storm, and, the moon being nearly hidden, the planet on which Christovao's eye was fixed with an almost impatient regard that it yet lingered on its course, gleamed out brightly. Zadig was engaged forming a kind of funeral pile of the wood he felled; and now, and again, did he ask the strange question of the man he meant to slay, " How goes the star ?"

From Christovao and the Moor anger had passed away. A single purpose was in their dark spirits; and to human eye, had such shared in the vulture's silent watch above them, they might have seemed friends. Nor were they enemies :—Montoyo felt not animosity towards his intended murderer, but thanked him for the death he awaited ;—and Zadig, by his faith in the immutable law of destiny, regarded the unhappy wretch before him as one who had but worked out his fate.

"How goes the planet?" again cried the Moor. He was hewing the last branch for the pile.

"It rests on the horizon," calmly answered the willing victim, his eyes still fixed on the gleaming orb, but dragging his bleeding frame nearer to Zuma's corse; "and now it sinks. It rises once again—it sinks—it sinks—'tis gone!"

"Die, then, Christovao de Montoyo!" exclaimed the Moor. He turned:—his scimitar plunged into the breast of the wounded man. The gathered storm burst over the river. The thunder roared, as though the battle of that day had found at length its echo in the skies: but Zadig stirred not from the task he had allotted to himself. The bodies of Christovao and Zuma he placed on the pile,—the means of ignition he bore about him; and, till their ashes were scattered by the morning breeze, the Moor fed the flame, and watched as by a watch-fire.

CHAPTER XXVI.

EXPLANATIONS.

The day after the disastrous battle of Alcazarquiver found the monarch of Portugal a wounded fugitive in an Arab Dowar; but Beatrice was with him, regarding his every look, and ministering to him with a tenderness which belongs alone to woman. The Marquis de Montoyo had made himself known to his daughter and to the King, but no time was afforded for the explanation of his long disappearance from the world, while they remained in the Arab tents; and to their inquiries respecting Zuma he gave no further reply than a repetition of the simple assertion that the Moorish girl was slain. He stated not that he had beheld her death ; and, carefully abstaining from the mention of Christovao's name, Beatrice was allowed to suppose that Zuma had fallen in the *melée* of the fight. Abdallah hastened their departure, though even the motion of a litter was agonizing to the wounded monarch ; but it was necessary for the safety of the fugitives that they should immediately leave their present locality, and this mode of carriage was the best they could afford him. Escorted by a body of Arabs, to whom their protector had become answerable for a large ransom, or rather remuneration ; the party, consisting of Sebastian, Beatrice, and the Marquis de Montoyo, accompanied by Abdallah, commenced their journey to the coast. Here it was the hapless King's intention, under the re-assumed name of Abrantes, to embark and return to Lisbon, for the purpose of making secret financial arrangements previously to leaving Portugal for ever.

" I have had enough of regal sway," said

Sebastian to his lovely companion, who, still in her page's costume, the exchange of which had proved so fatal to Zuma, rode beside his litter. " Had I used it only for my people's good, I might have shared a throne with thee, nor asked my peerless Beatrice to follow a fugitive through the wide world."

" My world goes with me when I go with thee," replied the blushing girl. " It is late to ask a father's sanction, but may we hope it will not be refused ?"

" Oh that thou hadst asked a brother's !" sorrowfully answered the Marquis de Montoyo ; " it had saved much evil : but let us make the past a lesson for the future. My sanction, my blessing, has long been thine ; it was given thee in the chapel of the Arabida."

" And on the morning of my flight from the Casa de Pena I beheld thee, father ?" said Beatrice eagerly.

" Yes, my child ; but little passed concern-, ing thee with which I was unacquainted. Would

I had still continued thine acknowledged guardian!" Then, turning to Sebastian, the old man thus addressed him : " When thou, my sovereign, didst unhappily believe the falsehoods of Da Camera, and I was dismissed the court, disgusted with the world, it seemed to me that I loved its vanities no longer."

" I have ever lamented my injustice to thee," interrupted Sebastian.

" Regret it not, sire : except that my bearing it so ill divided me from my family, it was well thy displeasure shut the gate to my ambition,—ambition that was ever to our house a bane and a temptation. My son ! my son !"

" What of Christovao ?"

" What of my brother ?"—burst simultaneously from the lips of his two auditors.

"If there is aught a faithful servant may claim from a royal master," said Montoyo solemnly, " let my son's name be never mentioned by us ;

and thou too, Beatrice, hear thy father's wish,—
let it be as if that son were dead."

" Thou shalt be obeyed," falteringly replied
Beatrice, who suddenly recollected the treason
of Christovao, which had been partially revealed
to her in the camp of Muley Moloch. She
looked towards Sebastian, and seeing, by his
surprise at the earnestness of the Marquis, that
he was unconscious of her brother's crime, she
felt thankful when the old man continued his
narrative. Beatrice shuddered at the thought
of again entering on the devious path of concealment ; but she felt that disclosing the treachery of one who had been so favoured, so
trusted, might, in Sebastian's present state,
have dangerously excited him.

" To turn from the Circean cup when its
dregs become bitter," said the Marquis de
Montoyo, " requires but little philosophy.
That I might be the chosen minister and adviser of the monarch who, as a boy, had been

my pupil,—though I trust in sincerity my counsel would have continued for his benefit,—had
been my darling ambition. In this I was disappointed, and I immediately secluded myself
in a Quinta on my estates at Oporto; and, after
arranging my affairs, entered into an Augustine
monastery. I had given up the guardianship
of my children at a time when they, most required my guidance, and bitterly have I been
punished for my error. Several years passed
over me in an abode of pious contemplation ;—
I had begun to feel a peace which belongs not
to this world; and excepting my occasional
compunction at having, I may truly say, deserted my family, the exercises of our holy religion solely occupied my thoughts. At length,
I heard that it had pleased your majesty to
dismiss from your counsels the Da Cameras.
These, my enemies, being removed from the
court, I felt that it was in my power to justify
my conduct, and with a King so generous as
yourself, be restored to royal favour. Then

did the strong demon of ambition again enter into my soul. I prayed against it,—I struggled with it,—but I found that my enemy was about to conquer me: and, that I might render impossible my return to the theatre of human affairs, without declaring myself an impostor to the world, I left the convent, so long my tranquil home, while, by my persuasion, the body of a monk just deceased was buried as the Marquis de Montoyo; my children being invited to attend his obsequies. Still, the latent passion for rule and aggrandizement belonging to my race, induced me to desire for my son the career of ambition I had thus closed on myself. My King knows how this was effected," said Montoyo hurriedly; " and it now only remains for me to say. that, determining to watch over the fortunes of my children, I became a recluse in the glen of the Arabida, and latterly one of the thirty religieux whom your majesty's care for the spiritual well-being of the army attached to the African expedition."

" Thanks, my more than father, for thy narrative," said Sebastian, who had so disposed his position in the litter that he was enabled to pay strict attention to the recital of the Marquis. " My beloved relative, Queen Catherine, was the last to believe thee guilty of the intrigues which the forgeries of the Da Cameras laid to thy charge ;—how would she now have rejoiced at thy exculpation ! Oh that thou hadst ever continued with me ! On the groundwork of noble sentiments, which it was thy unremitting study to establish in my heart, what a superstructure have I reared ! Thou hadst taught thy pupil to despise the effeminacy of the court, encouraging in me a manly inclination for athletic exercises ; and behold ! those whose interest it was to debase their sovereign, that they might rule his people, encompassed me with grooms, huntsmen, and bullfighters, while I was a mere child. So was my youth passed. But the memory of thy chivalrous lessons still remained to me, and I resolved to turn the

energy of character, in fostering which had been
thy delight, to nobler ends.   Again, hadst thou
been near me, I might have made my love of
warlike enterprise subservient to the interests of
my country.   But no! flatterers were around
me who promised me success in what I now
perceive to be a chimerical project.   It is true,
yesterday's field I might have won; but should
I have contented myself with the first step on
the throne of glory to which my expected con-
quests in Barbary were to lead me?   No! still
deaf to the remonstrances of sager counsel-
lors, the insidious plaudits of my immediate
associates would have stimulated me to push
forward; till my army, exhausted even by
repeated victories, must have fallen an easy
prey to the natives of the soil I invaded.   Oh
Montoyo! that one bearing thy name should
have been amongst the foremost in urging me
on this mad career;—and then, throughout the
battle which has proved my overthrow, so
mysteriously, so blindly act in favour of our

enemies! Had it been any other than Christovao, I should have pronounced him traitor; but no! he is inconsiderate and unskilled in war. I should have detected the fallacy of his advice during the whole expedition, had it not fanned the fire of my impetuosity; and his conduct in the fight was only the result of his misconceptions. It would have been better for me," sighed the monarch, " if thou, father, hadst continued my instructor, stemming the flood of my youthful ardour, which prevented the solid structure of a just and tranquil government being raised to the advantage of my people, than that he, for whom thou didst abdicate the marquisate, should have been my unfortunate adviser."

The painful feelings of Beatrice and the Marquis might have been betrayed to Sebastian, had he not, in consequence of the wound in his forehead, frequently closed his eyes, even when speaking. The father and daughter exchanged looks mutually soliciting silence on

the subject of Christovao's treason : the old
man now perceived this was not unknown to
Beatrice ; and a perfect understanding at an
early opportunity was established between the
relatives, that, till the King became convales-
cent, a circumstance so likely to excite him
should not be disclosed.

" When thy husband is able to bear such a
recital," said Montoyo, " I ask thee not to keep
this secret from him ; but oh ! speak not when
I am present.—Let me not hear the tale of my
son's dishonour."

During the day's journey Sebastian continued conversing with his two companions, or
rather, pouring forth his lamentations over.
the destruction he had brought on his gallant
army, the embarrassment of his kingdom, and
the expression of his regrets and self-accusa-
tions, apparently without seeking a reply. The
fond pressure of Beatrice's hand, passed through
the curtain of the litter, was a sufficient as-
surance of sympathy ; and the Marquis was too

well pleased in listening to these evidences of a subdued and contrite spirit to disturb the flow of discourse.

Travelling slowly, it was night ere our party had neared the sea-coast, where it was not deemed prudent actually to appear, till it had been ascertained if any of the Portuguese galleys were in the offing.

Since the arrival of the first fugitives from the battle, the fleet whfch had proudly landed the gallant army of Sebastian, had been, by the order of the governor of Arzilla, immediately broken up. Some returned to Europe, the bearers of evil tidings; while others cruised along the African coast for the purpose of succouring such of the discomfited Christians as gained the shores. It was in anticipation of this latter proceeding, that the King had suggested the feasibility of his embarking as a private Fidalgo belonging to the army, in any vessel which might appear off the part of the coast they had now approached.

Having avoided Arzilla, where he might have been recognized, he naturally imagined that the embarkation of a wounded officer, his page, and an ecclesiastic, could occasion little remark in the ship which might receive them, crowded as it would be with fugitives of every description fleeing from death or bondage. The tents of our wayfarers were now pitched about three miles from the sea, and Abdallah pushed forward with two Arabs to reconnoitre.

The fidelity of the Marabout to Sebastian and his companions in misfortune was ensured by the oath which he had made to succour the Donna Beatrice. The old man had, at first, regretted that he had undertaken to aid the escape of a Christian knight and priest, in addition to the protection he had pledged himself to afford a daughter of the house of Montoyo; but such was the noble bearing of the wounded general,—for of this rank did Sebastian appear to him,—that he soon, from inclination rather than the influence of his fair charge, exerted all his energies in behalf of the unhappy King. The old Marabout had, as well, found in the Marquis de Montoyo an occasional listener, to whom he could, in his usual didactic mode of discourse, put forth his dogmas as to the nothingness of life,—opinions in which Montoyo fully concurred ; nor were the Christian and the Mahomedan, on the general principle that " man disquieteth himself in vain," at issue. The philosophy of age and experience on this point generally takes the same complexion, as the giant mysteries of eternity throw their mighty shadows over the full of days.

Abdallah had not long departed for the coast, when a horseman, his steed covered with foam and spent with fatigue, arrived at the little encampment: it was Zadig. With much difficulty he had traced the route of the travellers, and he now sought occular evidence of his uncle's faithful discharge of the obligation he had imposed on him.

Beatrice and Montoyo were seated by Se-

bastian, in a tent which had, by Abdallah's
care, been divested in some degree of its rude
Arab character : by excluding their horses
from sharing the accommodation beneath the
goat-hair covering, greater space and comfort
were granted to the wounded man.   To seek
an interview with the Donna Beatrice, formed
no part of Zadig's intention.   He ascertained
that a reunion had taken place ; which, so far
as the supposed Dom Abrantes was concerned,
he had little difficulty in comprehending.   Beatrice was under the guardianship of her affianced husband.   She was, perhaps, already a
wife.   His hands so lately red with her brother's blood, he dared not appear before her ;—
he dared not even receive the thanks he might
fairly have claimed for having secured her, in
his uncle, a powerful protector from perils
which must otherwise have overwhelmed, not
only Beatrice, but also those for whose safety
she would have willingly forfeited freedom—
even life.

Had the grateful girl known that Zadig was among the tents, with what eagerness would she have sought him! Nor was it gratitude alone that enlisted her warmest sympathies in behalf of the Moor. He was the brother of Zuma,—Zuma, the sister of her heart ; whose death, amid the hurry and excitement of the last few days, she regarded as a sorrow too sacred to be indulged. No! rather would it become the treasured grief of years. Zadig was as well the prey of a hopeless passion which she had unhappily occasioned ; and this, acting on his ever distempered imagination, produced a morbid temperament of mind almost threatening insanity.

Beatrice was unacquainted with the immediate cause of Zuma's death ; the appalling fact that the Moorish girl had died in her stead, and by the hand of Christovao, never came to her knowledge : but the source of unhappiness she must still be to the brother of her friend, seemed, now that Zuma had left Zadig to the consolations of her sisterly affection, a fatality which nearly made her a convert to one of the Moor's favourite theories, that there are those whom, much as we may desire to benefit, we can only injure.

Zadig quitted the little Dowar, and Beatrice knew not that one to whom she was so deeply indebted had passed across the entrance of the tent, where, though little more than a listener to the suggestions of her husband and father, she was taking part in a serious conference. It was decisive of the locality and sphere of life in which this high-born Portuguese maiden should share the fortunes of a King, who, honestly adjudging himself incapable of governing, determined to retire into the repose of domestic privacy, and become as one dead to the world.

" Yes!" said Sebastian, " I will even follow the example thou didst set me, Marquis ; and, as I cannot withstand temptation, I will flee it: though I mean not to shelter myself within the walls of a monastery," continued the King, fondly smiling on his bride, for such he yet considered her.

" There is little need that thou shouldst, my son," responded the old Montoyo, who had, at Sebastian's request, reconciled himself to this parental mode of address. " Even I will be a partaker of the tranquil life which thou hast pictured to us; experience having proved to me that it is not by resigning the duties of society, we conquer our love for the world's ensnaring lusts. No! in humble reliance on Heaven, our best barrier against such tempta- tion is found in a life of usefulness to our fel- low-creatures, and the peaceful enjoyment of social blessings."

" Thou dost not speak, my Beatrice," said Sebastian, when the Marquis had ceased to address him. " Wilt thou consent to resign the throne I once asked thee to share?"

" Willingly, willingly," replied the fond girl, gently sinking into his arms, which closed over the fragile form that had withstood and suffered so much for his sake; while the old man parted her dark brown tresses, as they fell over the shoulder of her husband, and imprinted a kiss on the fair brow of his daughter.

" May he who made man, and woman to be a help meet for him, bless and keep both my children through life to eternity !" said Montoyo fervently.

A dark figure broke the moonbeam, which had till then been the only witness of the scene we have described.   The patriarch looked up; but, ere he could call the attention of Sebastian and Beatrice, the intruder had disappeared.

Zadig followed his uncle to the coast, where he found him making the necessary arrangements for the contemplated embarkation, with the commander of a vessel which, already nearly full of the unhappy fugitives of the Christian army, would sail for Lisbon the next

morning at day-break. This was in accordance
with the wishes of the King, as we have before
stated; and the Marquis de Montoyo had
there resources in his power more than sufficient to transmit the amount of their ransom,
and even supply their future wants, should
Sebastian's contemplated method of conducting these necessary arrangements prove in-
compatible with the preservation of his in-
cognito.

"I have performed my oath, Zadig," said
Abdallah, as the kinsmen together proceeded on
their homeward route towards the encampment.
"The son of my brother was wayward, but
I acted not towards him as a nurse with the
child she deceives by promises, soothing to the
ear, but lacking their fulfilment."

"Thou hast done well, mine uncle," replied
the young Moor; "thou hast repaid the daughter of the house of Montoyo for the sister's
love with which she did regard Zuma in her
captivity,—Zuma, who is now free as the ether

of eternity, — the atmosphere of immortal worlds."

"Thou didst not see the Donna, her affianced, and her sire, my son, in thy passage through the Dowar?" inquiringly remarked Abdallah, as Zadig relapsed into his accustomed musing.

"I saw them, kinsman; but I spoke not with them. The Senhor Abrantes knows me not; the Donna Beatrice has no pleasure in my presence; and the old man, her new found sire, may distrust me. 'Tis better that we meet not. To-morrow they will embark for Portugal; from thence they journey to the western Pyrenees: but now, I regarded them, — a happy group amid all their misfortunes, — I heard, too, their final destination named, 'In Andorra then will we make our future home, and we shall yet be happy!" It was the voice of Beatrice; — she spoke to her affianced husband!" exclaimed the Moor, with a burst of passionate excitement which might have startled any one less stoical than Abdallah, who calmly rejoined,

"Unrequited love is the beacon-fire of the heart which none hath answered. Quench it, or 'twill eat into the watch-tower. Why should it vex my son that a Christian maiden mates with a Christian knight? Art thou not a Mahomedan?"—Zadig was silent.—"Art thou not a Mahomedan? The faith of thy fathers should be thine."

"Kinsman, the creed I do profess might only anger thee didst thou know it," at length replied Zadig.

"I am past the hour of wrath: say on: hast thou no faith in Mahomed, my son?"

"As I have faith in thee, father," answered the young Moor. "He lived as thou dost live,—he died as thou must die,—the destiny that was allotted him he fulfilled. The founder of all creeds I worship,—that was, and is, and is to be. The fashioner of space—eternity, —who speaketh by the stars; who hath all

power, save power to blot that which his om-
niscience hath writ. There! I have angered
thee," continued Zadig, as Abdallah stayed his
horse, and stretched out his long, attenuated
arm toward heaven.

"Son," solemnly replied the old man,
"Allah is angry with thee. I am not worthy
to espouse a cause so sacred. Thou dost re-
ject the Koran. When yon Christians leave
these shores, thou shalt go with me to Mecca;
there, at the Prophet's tomb, the light of true
belief may visit thee."

"I follow the Christians," doggedly replied
Zadig.

"And break thy faith with thy father's brother? But few days have passed since thou
saidst the desert should be thine abiding-place,
the mountain of Djibbel Habeeb thy fenced
city, and the sons of our tribe thy brethren.
Thou hast lied unto me, Zadig," reproachfully but calmly remarked the old man, as
he again put his horse to the gentle pace their

steeds had kept during the foregoing conversation.

"Who says Zadig has broken his plighted word?" demanded the young Moor, scornfully throwing back the accusation. "I told thee there was one to whom I would say farewell, even the bard Camoens: I follow the Donna Beatrice when I visit the master who loved me, bore with me gently, made me his companion, friend, while I was yet his bondsman; and, though his last wealth was in possessing me, by Camoens I was made free. Kinsman, he hath not long to live: the coldness of the world had chilled the springs of life when we parted. I shall return to him, nor yet will break my faith with thee. Again I renew my pledge; ere another year hath in its revolution passed the celestial signs, I shall have done with Europe. Then will I seek thee, an thou like it, even at the Prophet's tomb. Thou art no bigot to constrain my creed; I will adore with thee—not Mahomed, but Allah,—worship

and praise and magnify; do aught but pray,
—'twere vain to pray the power that hath
ordained!"

And here Zadig, to prevent further reply on
the part of his uncle, dashed forward on the
road they were pursuing. Abdallah continued
his quiet course; and in a few moments after
his impetuous kinsman galloped back, holding
out his hand to the Marabout.

"We are friends; we understand each other
now, my father," said Zadig.

"There is friendship between us," responded
the old man, accepting the proffered overture
of amity. "Thou dost understand *me;* to
understand *thee* is a task too hard for me at
present."

Zadig again rode by the side of Abdallah,
and together they reached the tents, where, by
the desire of the young Moor, his presence in
the little encampment was carefully concealed
from the knowledge of their guests. At day-
break the party proceeded to the coast; Zadig

still keeping himself from the observation
of Beatrice and the Marquis de Montoyo.
Ere the sun had risen, Sebastian with his
companions embarked ; and the Moor turned
from the shore but to await the approach of
the first vessel which might follow on the track
of the voyagers.

CHAPTER XXVII.

THE FUGITIVE KING.

We have accompanied Sebastian from the period of his landing on the shores of Africa, strong in the consciousness of youth and health, elate in hope, confident of conquest, and at the head of a gallant army; until the moment when, a wounded fugitive, whose name had already passed from the earth, he departed from that country to subjugate which he had tempted Fortune.

Where now the brave nobles who had followed their royal master to the field of Alcazarquiver,—chiefs and scions of honourable houses, the pride of Lusitania? Where now the gathered warriors of Germany, Italy, Portugal, and Castile? —"In one red burial blent!"

Of the whole invading army, about fifteen thousand men, it is calculated not three hundred escaped slaughter; and the greater portion of these, being captured without hope of ransom, pined out a miserable existence amid the toils and degradation of slavery. One historian estimates the number of those saved from carnage at fifty only; but, on comparing several other accounts of the battle, we are inclined to keep to our original statement. The loss sustained by the Moors was enormous; nineteen thousand followers of Mahomed forming hecatombs of slain to the manes of the Christians, who had thus during the action destroyed several thousand beyond their own numerical force at its commencement.

When it is considered that the invaders were worn by toilsome marches across burning sands; scantily supplied with food and water; exposed to a glowing African sun by day, and indifferently sheltered from the noxious dews of night, ere they opposed an army four times their force, well may the old chroniclers of Portugal declare that their compatriots "worked a miracle in their martyrdom on the bloody field of Alcazarquiver!"

It is generally agreed that, together with other unhappy circumstances which induced the failure of the expedition, treason was not inactive in the camp of Sebastian. Muley Moloch was acquainted with everything that passed in the counsels of the Portuguese; and the reader need not be informed that among those who betrayed their King and his gallant warriors on the shore of Africa was Christovao de Montoyo. It is not our intention to follow the fugitive monarch to Lisbon. That he was among the survivors of the fight many contemporary historians plainly assert, and these accounts are only contradicted by partisans of the Spanish faction—whose aim it was to make Portugal a province of Spain,—and some later chroniclers biassed by their misrepresentations. The body declared to have been that of the King was in the first instance made the instrument of deceit by a Fidalgo of the name of Figuéra, though with the most loyal intention. According to the reverend brother, Joseph Texere, Prior of the monastery of Santerem, a diligent inquirer into the matter,-" this officer had parted with Sebastian about four leagues from the field of battle, to ascertain if the enemy continued in pursuit; and, after a while returning the same way to seek the King, he fell into the hands of the Moors. On their questioning him as to his royal master, Figuéra, to the end that they should desist from further search, told them that he saw his body lying among the dead." Again, the same grave authority assures us that he was informed by the son of Muley Hamet, who after his father's death became a Christian, and lived for many years in Spain, bearing the hollow title of Prince of Morocco, that " Sebastian, the King, withdrew himself from the battle, embarked in his galiot, and, for a certainty, was alive."

The Prior goes on then to state what passed in a conference between him and the brother of Muley Hamet, Cid Albequerin, which took place in Lisbon, about the second month after the disastrous issue of the expedition; proving Sebastian, though severely wounded, to have survived the fight. But, not to weary the reader, we will duly state the means taken by Philip of Spain to strengthen the supposition that Sebastian was slain; and then proceed to show, from good authority, that the fugitive King of Portugal actually returned to Lisbon. Antonio, Prior of Crato, Sebastian's kinsman, was among the few survivors of the battle; and, with the young Duke of Barcelos, became prisoner to the Moors. Though the Prior ultimately disputed the throne of Portugal with Philip, it was his policy, at that time, to appear in the interests of the Spanish monarch;

he thus readily confirmed the mistake his captors had made in supposing they were possessed of Sebastian's body; and found means of communicating to the court of Madrid, the course affairs had taken. In the mean time, the alleged royal corse, which the best authorities during the remainder of that century declare to have been the body of a Swiss adventurer in Stukeley's free company, had been embalmed and placed under charge of a noble Moor in the city of Alcazarquiver.

Philip's policy was doubtless to gain possession of these relics of mortality, and treat them in every respect as the veritable remains of Sebastian. Thus he deputed an accredited minister to the new Emperor of Morocco, proposing terms of alliance, which, as a preliminary, required the ransom of the Prior Crato, the Duke of Barcelos, and the supposed corse of the Portuguese King. Succeeding in his embassy, this ambassador conveyed his sacred trust to Ceuta, demanding a receipt from the governor of that town for the same: in due course it was forwarded to Lisbon, and, in the month of January 1583, the body was buried in the convent of Belem, three miles below Lisbon, as our records express, " with much honour, fasting, and solemn pomp."

The day of this politic funeral was marked at Madrid by masses and religious processions; while Philip, determined that Sebastian, alive or dead, should never again reign in Portugal, beheld with satisfaction the sceptre of that kingdom fall into the possession of the half imbecile sensualist Dom Henry.

At the decease of the quondam Cardinal, the sovereign power became vested in the throne of Castile; death, in the short space of thirty years, having removed twelve reigning monarchs and heirs of the blood royal, to make way for the ambitious Philip.

We shall now hasten to conclude this relation of the expedition to Barbary, by giving as our authority for asserting that Sebastian returned to Lisbon after the battle of Alcazar-quiver, " an addition of some importance (so announced) to a work containing " a discourse concerning the success of the King of Portugal, Dom Sebastian, from the time of his voyage into Africa, when he was lost (disappeared) in the battle against the infidels, in the year 1578, unto the 6th of January this present 1601 : all done into Spanish, then into French, and now lastly translated into English."

To this curious record we have been much indebted during the progress of our story. It is there stated that " Sebastian and others did all secretly and strangely disguise themselves, that they could not be known to any one; which being done, the King and they, in the confused return of the army to Portugal, came back with *them*, where having bound the rest to him by a dear engaged oath that none of them would be seen or known, but providing themselves of such jewels and gold as they could conveniently get, departed all again from Portugal.   The King said, ' His grief and shame was so great that by his folly and rashness the Christians were discomfited, and suffered so mighty a loss, to the hurt of all Christendom ; therefore he would no more be seen.' "

CHAPTER XXVIII.

THE DYING BARD.

Our *dramatis personæ* have been gathered together by some of those strange incidents which might be confessed to belong as much to reality as fiction, were every extraordinary reunion in the " thousand and one" romances of real life recorded. Again they are scattered : the Moorish girl has found that rest which the world denied her ; — the dark spirit of Christovao is gone down to the shadows of death. He who, gloating over fancied injuries, had lived but for vengeance,—died by the hand of the avenger. Sebastian, Beatrice, and the ancient Marquis de Montoyo have for a while passed from the scene of our story : we will continue with Zadig, and accompany him to Portugal. He waited long ere he could obtain a passage, and at length proceeded to Tangiers for that purpose; the old Marabout having taken leave of him by the way, on Zadig's repeating his promise of a speedy return. Embarking from thence for the Tagus, he arrived in Lisbon, and rested not till he had found out his old master.

· Camoens was in far greater poverty than when the Moor had left him. Then, it is true, the superfluities of life were denied, but there yet remained. food and raiment; while that which robing and sustenance were to the body, the mind still held in possession, despite misfortune, — hope, to feed and clothe the soul. Though its daily garnish of fair fruit, like the apple of the Dead Sea shore, became ashes, and the green leaves of promise withered with the setting sun, the morning renewed them :—now, no renewal came !

Such was the substance of Camoens' welcome to the Moor, who found him in an obscure lodging within the western suburb of Lisbon.

"Ah, Zadig! I am now poor indeed," continued the bard, pursuing the theme of his increased misery; "food, raiment, hope, all gone, — even shelter is to be denied me! My last coin is expended! I thought all had abandoned me, and that to-morrow I must have been cast forth to die in the street, or, perchance, carried to an hospital. The broken chalice which contains the dregs of life were better crushed at once than perish thus: but in those dregs a pearl exists no poison can destroy; 'twill rise again to gem the courts of Heaven: —such is my belief, Zadig. Hast thou in thy strange creed, made up of chaotic elements, confounding mystery with mystery, a better soul-sustaining hope when the worn frame is tottering o'er that gulf where nature shrinks from that which is most natural — from death?"

" Master,"_ answered Zadig, evading the question, which he knew was but a gauntlet thrown down inviting argument, " it is with life we have to do, not death. How wilt thou live on with lack of bread, when disease is feeding on thy wasted powers? Have all means been tried to awaken the compassion of the court? Was it to die near the abode of the rich and proud, the high of birth, they lured Portugal's only bard with the mockery of a pension?"

" Even so, Zadig: my name still swells the courtly retinue. Sebastian dead, I shall be considered the pensioner of Dom Henry; allowed admittance to the presence-chamber, could I crawl there, and yet denied the paltry pittance that would gain me food. My meals have often now a grace more solemn than prayer or thanksgiving,—a yesterday of fasting !"

" Dear master," exclaimed the Moor, " this must not be :" and his broad chest heaved with emotion as he gazed on the pallid face of Camoens, o'er which a smile played, though it was but a sad one. The smile of the blind is ever painful to the beholder, for the brightness which should illume it is not there, and the bard was then rapidly losing the sight of that eye which had directed the labours of his immortal pen : thus threatening to involve one, who mentally had been the only light which had risen for ages over the intellectual gloom of Portugal, in perfect night.

That Camoens' vivid fancy should yet return, and its scintillations burst forth, even at his own distresses, need not surprise us. Camoens had been taught by affliction to become a Christian philosopher ; and Misfortune had so long made her home with him, that she was familiar as a friend. Not even when disturbed by intrusion on the privacy of his thoughts,—when visited by those who sought the gratuitous offices of his muse, while they withheld the assistance which might long have kept on earth the soul of the immortal genius whose aid they craved,—could he be aroused to anger.

A Fidalgo, named Ruy Dias da Camera, was the last who came to his miserable dwelling on this ungracious errand. He requested the poet to translate into Portuguese for him the Penitential Psalms, and Camoens thus expressed himself in answer to his solicitations:

" When I wrote verses, I was young and had sufficient food ; was a lover, and beloved by many friends :—thus I felt poetic ardour. Now I am without energy.—Behold ! I require two vintems to buy coal, and I have them not."

His appeals to the ministers of Dom Henry had been equally manly and affecting, but subdued. His disease, aggravated by want of nourishment, long prevented him from leaving his lodgings: his letters to the court were unanswered, and he remained untended and unvisited. The return of Zadig, and the devoted attachment he expressed for Camoens, cheered the desolate sufferer; but he at once saw the improbability of assistance from such a source.

"And how art thou to obtain the bread thou talkest of?" said the bard, in reply to the young Moor's anxious proffers of service. "Labour will be denied thee; none but the Moorish slave will now have work: added to *his* toil will be the task refused his free compatriots; for prejudice runs strong against thy race, and she ever visits on the innocent the wrongs the guilty have committed. Muley Moloch and his Arab hordes have shed the dearest blood of Portugal amid the plains of Alcazarquiver; and here, in Lisboa, every citizen doth think he righteously avengeth this great ruin, by heaping chains and injuries on the Moor by sad captivity long naturalized in Lusitania. No, Zadig — thou must quit this land, and seek thy fortune on some distant shore:—thou couldst not gain me bread, even didst thou beg for it."

"Beg for it!" exclaimed Zadig: " master,

it shall be so. I ask but tribute from those who tribute owe, and have forgotten payment. This night will I to the bridge of Alcantara, conceal my Moorish dress beneath yon ragged cloak, and subsidize thy countrymen, who, to their shame, have left thee thus to perish."

" My friend," said Camoens, raising himself from his couch, " the act were vain; I want not bread now :—no longer do I care for corporeal food ;—my spirit already anticipates the high banquet of immortality.   Zadig !"—His call was unanswered.

" The impetuous Moor had fled ; and that evening a stranger importuned the passengers, who were returning from a festa held at the convent of Belem, with the unchanging cry of " Bread for Camoens !"

The appeal was an affecting one ; but the Moor threw an authoritative and reproachful expression into his demand, of which he felt conscious, though he tried in vain to conquer so injudicious a manifestation of feeling. When he applied to a single Fidalgo, the alarmed wayfarer's eyes would glance from Zadig's commanding form in search of some fellow-passenger, lest violence might be offered him. Crowds would pass by unheedingly, and many sneered at the sturdy beggar:—but one old man asked how fared Camoens. This was an idle question, yet it bespoke sympathy; and Zadig told of his master's abject want. The citizen of Lisbon shook his head, and sapiently remarked,

" Poetry is a useless trade; no good can come of it; but here are two vintems."

It was the sole benefaction the Moor received: and the passengers becoming more and more scattered as night drew on, at length he was left the only occupant of the bridge of Alcantara. With a sum in value about the fifth part of a shilling, laid out to the best advantage in bread, wine, and fruit, Zadig returned to Camoens. The bard had been sleeping, and just then awoke: with a faint voice, he addressed the Moor:

" Thou hast put thyself to much prostration of spirit, my friend, to beg for me."

" I felt none, master, for I was indignant at the dastard, niggard wretches," answered Zadig; " but that I feared my possible detention might have left thee again forsaken, I would have *made* them answer my demand.   Partake of this bread, good Senhor; here is some wine too."

" I will partake of both, if only to show my gratitude to thee, Zadig," replied the bard; " yet there is that within me,—a sinking of the frame,—a prescience of the soul,—which tells me I shall want little more of food.   I shall not burthen thee long, my friend.   Some dark slab in the church of Santa Anna for a while displaced, and the perishing fragments of mortality beneath will be all Camoens need disturb. The Padrés, though they all, even to the brotherhood of the Benedictines, have forgotten me, must, for the love of God, perform my funeral rites. It is likely, when thou askest them to do so, Zadig, they may remember that I died unshriven. But why should I ask their intercessions with the Deity who bids the suppliant draw near to him through one mediator, Christ the Saviour? Zadig, thou lookest displeased: thou dost not like my creed, though I have overthrown a thousand saints to simplify it. Thy god is destiny; and him who did ordain, thou makest subservient to the power he created,—dethroning his omnipotence. 'Tis a strange and dangerous doctrine; but thou art so stubborn in thy belief, I do fear me there is little chance my arguments will cause thee to see its fallacy."

" Master," replied Zadig, " our creeds are neither fashioned nor laid by at will; they are the pinions on which the soul soars into unseen worlds ;—or dark or bright their plumage, they take not hue and order at our bidding. Re-

cords or traditions some may satisfy, yet, 'mid
a hundred creeds one only can be right; and
thus the hope of Heaven or Hell, the code
of human obligation to the Deity, influencing
the eternal destiny of millions, must be false:
and, knowing this with the poor intellect allowed me, I think I have read aright my doctrine of fate immutable. The old man who
was my teacher in my youth did speak to me of
much I now believe, though not of all. He
had been a worshipper of huge serpents, said
to have lived for untold ages in Egyptian
sanctuaries; the living temples of the eternal
spirit, until his progress in the celestial science
rolled back the clouds that had hidden light
and revelation. But I do weary thee, my
master; it is time that thou shouldst sleep."

" I want not sleep, Zadig, and freely listen
to thee, though I mourn thy visionary wandering. The creed that amid the wreck of nations,
tongues, and even creeds, hath stood the test
of ages, is of the cross of Christ. In this be-

lief I die. Oh! it is happiness to know that faith hath power to make the miserable on earth the inheritor of eternal bliss! Now give me that cup of wine, and sit thee near me."

The Moor hastened to obey Camoens, who, tasting the beverage, offered it to his companion.

" Drink, Zadig;—the poison of disease is not on my lips. It is true that I am dying; but my frame hath yet the energies of years in it. I have heard, the lust of life—the strong desire to live—doth sometimes give reanimation to the sick whom the sage mediciner hath pronounced as on the bed of death. *My* soul has wearied of this earth, nor will it lend the vital spark to longer bondage. I have already lived too long: I look for fellowship in vain,—friends I have none save thee. Ah! Catherina, Heaven is thy fitting home; soon shall I join thee in those realms of bliss. And thou, Antonio! friend of my youth, sharer of every thought, and comrade in fields of toil and danger,—yes!

we shall meet within the world of spirits, and
from the realms of space regard this sublu-
nary scene; amid the wonders of revolving
spheres, with all the secret springs of essence
and of matter bared to eyes opened on immortality, still pondering one mystery,—how
man, who feels that he doth journey to eternity, can toy with life as though it led but to
annihilation."

Camoens, after having thus apostrophized the
mistress and friend of his early days, Donna
Catherina de Atayde, and Dom Antonio de
Noronha, seemed to have forgotten that Zadig
was present. For a while he appeared engaged
in mental prayer; and his faithful attendant,
finishing a sparing meal, prepared himself to
sleep on the ground at a little distance from
the poet's bed.

Several months passed, during which Camoens was supported by Zadig's exertions;
now as a water-carrier, braving the taunts of a
city rabble; now, on the festival days of the

many churches about Lisbon, importuning the passengers for charity; but ever returning at night to the bard, whose vital energies were sinking fast.

Camoens had resigned himself to death, and patiently awaited its coming. His lamentation was for his country. The pride of her manhood slain, her resources drained; a bigot imbecile on the throne, and the Inquisition spreading its cancerous fibres throughout Portugal, even unto Goa: these national calamities affected him with a deeper sorrow than the penury and disease which were hastening his appeal from the "tender mercies" of ungrateful Lusitania, to the high court of Heaven.

It was about the tenth month after Zadig had taken on himself the charge of Camoens,—whom all others seemed to have forgotten,—that the Moor had the mortification of returning home, without even the coarse food which had till then sustained these companions in misery. Supperless had they gone to their hard beds, for Zadig had not that day earned enough to procure a meal. Heavily the bard slept, but the eyes of his watchful friend were ever opening to regard the sick man. The chimes of the church of Santa Anna told the hour of midnight, when Zadig started from the ground.—Camoens had called him by name. Seated upright in the bed, his eye dilated, and beaming with a strange lustre which seemed to absorb the rays of the solitary taper placed near him, the bard fixedly regarded the Moor. One hand was resting on the pillow, supporting him in his upraised position, and with the other he slowly beckoned.

" Zadig," said Camoens, " I have been in a trance."

" No, master ; thou hast but slept," quickly answered his alarmed attendant.

" I have been in a trance, Zadig," solemnly reiterated the dying man, " and I have seen a vision mingling earth and heaven. I had been ages dead, if bliss like that I felt we may call death, and had in spirit come to hover o'er the earth. Princes and people, sages and bards, a gathering of nations were calling on Camoens. That fame, winging its way through Christendom, for which my soul in life had panted, now was mine. Honour to Camoens!—every tongue joined in the song of praise. Amid this strange apotheosis I heard a seraph's voice, and thus it spake: 'Wilt thou return to earth?' The wings that bore me trembled; but I answered, 'Rather be mine with humble strain to swell our loud hosannahs round the celestial throne.' "

The poet's eye grew dim. " Zadig!"—his head bowed toward the Moor: the hand which had grasped his, relaxed its pressure; and the soul of the bard of Lusitania passed to the realm of spirits. His incidental mention of the convent of Santa Anna determined the last resting-place of Camoens. It was the nearest religious house to the shed which had sheltered the dying bard. Here, beneath a marble slab, were deposited the mortal remains of the author of the Lusiad, undistinguished from the humblest unlettered peasant of Portugal; his obsequies unattended, as his death was unlamented, by all save one faithful attendant.

CHAPTER XXIX.

CONCLUSION.

AMIDST the wildest and most picturesque scenery of the eastern Pyrenees, still exists the little federate republic of Andorra. The continuance of these peaceful vales for many centuries in undisturbed possession of ancient rights and privileges, though it would seem without guardianship save in the lofty peaks which like giants of the earth kept court around, is in itself a wonder. Leaving this extraordinary fact to the consideration of statesmen and politicians, nor feeling called on to trace this political phenomenon from the wars of Charlemagne even to the days of Sebastian, and again bring down its history to our later times, we will at once plunge into the deep valleys, and climb the mountain crags of Andorra; finding our wonders in the works of One, to whom man, weaving his finite web of policy, is as the summer spider, which a breath wafts away, shrouded in the fabric it hath woven.

From north to south, and from east to west, the traveller can journey little more than thirty miles in this mimic state; which is bounded on the four cardinal points by Arriege, Urgal, Paillas, and Carol: yet, in this confined arena, arise several of the highest summits from among the Pyrenees. Behold yon peak, gaunt and bare,—as if maddened by the glories revealed where the sun is without a cloud;—it scorns the green dress of earth, till at mid-height the glad foliage clasps around its rugged sides. The pine bows to the oak in reverence to the ancient of ages; and the graceful bindweed flings her tendrils from crag to crag, dressing the mountain monarch to meet his lowland bride. The torrent sings a joyous melody of rushing waters, as the vale of Es-caldos receives her lord into her bosom. The active izard bounds away from the haunts of man;—in the silvery stream murmuring through the valley, the glistening trout darts by; while, ever and anon, is heard the whistling rush of birds, as bursting the dense thickets of olive and pomegranate, they wing their flight into the blue ether.

It was evening; and at the base of the moun-tain we have described, might be remarked a pretty cottage built after the Switzer's fashion: an ample roof overhung its low walls, and stretched out in many radiations from a centre, where tall chimneys told that Andorra's winter was not without rigour, though summer just then, in warmth and beauty, shone around. An abundantly stocked mountain homestead open-ed its gates in the distance, while gardens en-compassed the little domain even to the rising ground: here nature, in playful mood, seemed struggling with cultivation; rendering the half reclaimed wilderness akin to the deep ravine and sylvan glen, from which crags, and rocks, and fantastic peaks rose in the silence·of that stilly eve.

A hunter in the pride of manhood, who had been in chase of the izard since morning, was within sight of this happy home. In fancy he could people the cottage porch,—where the vine and myrtle seemed striving which should possess it for a bower,—with a familiar group watching for his return. Nor was this a day-dream of the imagination.

An aged man was seated in that porch; a sacred volume resting on his knees, which would have been more attentively perused but for the endearments of a lovely child, who clambered by his side,—now twisting his tiny fingers in his old grandsire's locks, now bringing his rosy cheek close to the wrinkled brow of age, ringing out again and again childhood's free and joyous laugh ;—glad sounds which had yet even a fonder listener than yon grey old man.

· The mother of that cherub boy was there ; her dark eyes beaming with delight as she gazed on her first-born ;—and then with anxious look, taking in its circuit miles of the mountain range, she would endeavour to trace, in the far distance, the venturous track of her returning husband.

Leaving the vale, we will make ourselves companions of the hunter, who, though pursuing his homeward course, had yet more than a long mile to travel ere he joined the happy group at the cottage door. His green jerkin was fitted closely to an athletic form where strength and activity appeared well blended : he grasped a long iron-shod staff in his right hand, and over his shoulder was thrown a full-grown izard ; while, bounding by his side, two large dogs of the deer-hound breed, seemed by their loud bark and frequent rough caresses to claim that companionship with their master, which a salutary fear of the staff alone prevented from being rather dangerous amid the passes our cragsman was descending. But the sagacious animals on the sudden ceased their gambols :— uttering a cry, which to the practised ear of the hunter told that a stranger was at hand, they dashed forward, and in a few minutes returned, ushering into his presence a swarthy-looking traveller, who had apparently crossed the mountain, and lost the direct path to the valley.

"Down Wolf! Down Hector! To heel, hounds!" exclaimed the mountaineer, calling back his dogs, which seemed craving permission to tear the wayfarer to the earth. Silently the stranger acknowledged the courtesy of their master, whom he was now regarding with an agitated scrutiny, which might have called forth a rebuff, had not the party subjected to his wild gaze been just then busily engaged, securing the fiercer of the dogs in a leash. When the sportsman raised his head to greet the traveller, a countenance presented itself to him where the deeply traced lineaments seemed chiselled in dark marble, so motionless had they become after one slight convulsive ebullition of feeling had passed away.

" Thou art not a hunter, and yet in the hunter's track," said the mountaineer. " If thou art willing, I will be thy guide to the vale, for to proceed onward will lead thee to destruction. Thou wilt be lost amid the crags, where a false step may be thy death."

" Thanks, friend," said the wayfarer; " yet to-night I journey across to Encampo; it is but àn angle of the mountain, and the path seems clear. But why art *thou* so late in these wilds? is thy home at hand ?"

" Ay, gallant stranger," rejoined the cragsman ; " it is now barely half a mile to my cottage : come with me, and thou shalt share its cheer. See ! the road winds along the side of yon rock; when we have passed that point, our destination will be just beneath us. I saw it ere we met, but those trees have just hidden it from our view. Say, wilt thou go with me? It is late to journey to Encampo."

" Yet there I sleep to-night, if aught of sleep may visit one who hath but little communion with that power by which the doomed, the worker of his destiny, forgets that he is wretched. Walk on,—I follow thee," said the gaunt traveller, wrapping his sad-coloured cloak around him, which seemed worn and travel-stained.

" I shall be glad if thou wilt partake of rest and refreshment in my cottage," responded the mountaineer, smiling at the extraordinary vehemence of his companion; "but there was a time when I brooked not the sharp tone in which it is thy pleasure to indulge."

" Bear with me," replied the stranger, " a moment more, and we shall part." The deep dejection of manner with which this request was uttered admitted not of a denial: silently they proceeded, the hunter wondering much at the excited bearing of the traveller, until, winding round a ravine, the valley lay before them.

Already had the joyful husband waved his cap to the expectant wife, who held on high their boy to greet his father. The old man too had risen, and, sustained by a staff, joined the young mother in welcoming the sportsman after his day of toil; for, almost forgetful of his invited guest, he had sprung forward. Seeking the chase but for exercise, and the remembrance of other days, he returned to his home with re-doubled zest after its wild excitement was past. But where was the stranger? — Mounting a crag which overhung the vale, as the hunter, threading a little glen, had emerged on the green sward within a few yards of the cottage,— he lifted his arms to heaven, invoking blessings on the scene before him. His tall form was poised, as if toppling on the brink of the preci-pice, when a cry of delight and astonishment

arose from beneath. The wayfarer had been
recognised, and a kindly welcome awaited him
from one who knew not that the blood of a
brother was on his hands;—but he turned and
fled. The peaceful homestead in the valley of
Escaldos contained the household of Sebastian.
The stranger was Zadig the Moor.

THE PIRATE ISLAND.

THE PIRATE ISLAND.

PART FIRST.

In the Bay of Amboazes, on the Camaroon coast of western Africa, is an insulated rock, which Nature has decked so verdantly, that, lured by the waving palms and plantains which seemed to beckon them, many natives from the neighbouring shores have made it their habitation. Situated scarcely more than a cable's length from the mainland, where the densely wooded coast, after running a while its level course, mounts proudly to an elevation of thirteen thousand feet, humbly does the little island appear to wait at the footstool of the mighty Camaroons,—as a slave at a divan of kings.

With a few scattered rocks on either hand it
can alone claim fellowship in insignificance;
though, doubtless sprung of ancient convul-
sion, it may boast common birth with the adjacent mountains,—even to the more distant Qua,
whose lofty head pierces the clouds, like some
rebellious giant of the earth that would read
the secrets of the skies. But, lowly as this rock
of the ocean may seem among the more majes-
tic works of Nature's hand in the Bay of Amboazes, it is still a most picturesque object. The
mimic isle is only a mile and a half in circum-
ference: precipitate scoria cliffs present themselves on every side,—as if to prevent access
to a crowd of conically roofed huts that thickly
stud the grassy level of the lower heights;
— on the opposite side of the island rises a
fantastic little peak crowned by lofty palms;
its overhanging sides decked with luxuriant
wreaths of creeping and pendent plants,—whilst
below, resting on the tranquil waters, the fish-
ing canoes of the natives are half embayed by

the scattered rocks around, wrought into natural arches and tunnels, and taking every form
and fashion to the eye of fancy.

About one hundred and fifty natives make
this islet their habitation ; and, albeit an abode
that bears an evil name, the deeds of these simple and inoffensive Africans have not entitled it
to the appellation by which it is distinguished.
Yet are there some of the ancient of days
among the islanders who tell strange tales of
rapine and blood, and of treasure hidden amid
the recesses of the cliffs ; and, though twelve
times a hundred " moons" have waned since
the white man made here his home of violence,
still its designation may be traced to European
crime ; for it was the daring exploits of a band
of adventurers in the early part of the last century, who had made this isolated spot, as well
as the coast adjacent, their rendezvous, which
caused, in after years, this verdant rock of the
ocean to become known as the Pirate Island.

The events we have on record must, in the

first instance, carry the reader back to the year
1700. We have been enabled to be thus far
chronologically correct, having accidentally discovered a connection between the incidents of
the Pirate Island and the annals of an ancient
family in the west of England; and, that our
tale may be more clearly elucidated, we must
for a while quit the shores of Africa, and trans-
port ourselves to the Landsend of Cornwall.

Our scene opens a few miles to the westward
of Penzance: on that promontory where the
bold cliffs and craggy headlands of our native
England stretch forth in the proud and stupen-
dous order of Nature's architecture;—seeming,
as they rear their granite walls high above the
roaring waters of the vast Atlantic, to frown the
mandate of their Creator's power, " Here let
thy waves be stayed!" If the reader has ever
visited the extraordinary scenery of Botalloch
and Cape Cornwall, he need not be reminded
of the uncultivated waste which there surrounded him. Undecked but by the stunted

fern, and encumbered by large masses of moor-stone, it would appear as if some dragon-guardian of metallic treasure, in opening to man the yawning mine, had breathed upon the earth ; and the once contented tiller of the ground,—returning from the caverns in which was stored the tempting ore,—found the green herb had drooped and died. The election once made, the husbandman became lost in the miner, and the " ground was accursed for his sake." Yet even here the reaping-hook and scythe are at times wielded in some more favoured spot, where the industry of man, relieving the earth from the pressure of the sterile rock, has taken from the soil the curse of barrenness.

It is of such an oasis of the Landsend,—a few green fields where verdure is heightened by contrast with the scene around,—that it is our province to speak. About three miles from the promontory of Cape Cornwall, in the midst of several acres of arable and pasture land, a wall of great thickness, rising in its centre into a small ivy-clad tower,—the column of an ancient chimney,—gives support to the mud-built gable-ends and fern-thatched roof of a cow-lodge.

This erection is now the appurtenance of a farm-house in the neighbourhood, that would seem to boast the origin of the surrounding cultivation : but long before that homestead was reared there were pastures, and corn-fields, and even gardens, at Bostavern ; while the corner-stones of the supporting wall, and the granite masses rudely piled to uphold the open front of the shed referred to, bear marks of the workman's tool, which render it apparent they were squared and fashioned to take part in an edifice of prouder pretension than a covering for the beasts of the field. The once gay parterre has disappeared, but some few plants of a garden-race yet claim, as if by feudal tenure, the shelter of the ruin they smile on in its fallen fortunes ; for they are seedlings of flowers that had decked a home of happiness,—gladdening

with their beauty and fragrance the ancient residence of Richard Lanyon.

" Why dost thou build the hall, son of the winged days ?"
OSSIAN.

About eighty years ago, the mansion of which
we speak, even then a ruin, afforded material
for the building of the adjacent farm-house ;
and with the refuse of its walls were fenced
lands,—once the gardens and pleasant places of
their founder. There, however, still remains a
solitary pile in which is caverned the hearth of
that hall where, by the crackling blaze, the
Christmas carol has been sung, and the winter's
tale told, and the stranger was welcome as a
son at his father's board : yet even this is
now defiled by the strong team that has drag-
ged the plough where man had made unto himself a home, and said in his pride, " I shall
not be moved." But, as with the wand of
an enchanter, the annalist of other days must
rear again the walls that are fallen, and must

breathe the breath of life into the dead:—Bostavern must arise in all the rude comfort of
former days;—its familiar forms and voices
must be recalled; and the life, and light, and
beauty must return, of a generation long passed
away.

It was a lovely evening that had lent the
glow and splendour of a tranquil sunset to a
somewhat stormy day; and the blazing fire in
the large oak-panelled hall of Bostavern bore
witness that, though winter had not yet arrived,
autumn was hastening that period so dear to
domestic happiness, when elemental rigour
seems to draw nearer and dearer the ties of
home. Great was the surprise and annoyance
of Mr. Lanyon, that his daughter Mary had
not yet made her appearance at their evening
meal. Mary was his favourite child; and
though a blooming girl and boy were seated on
either side of his placid and still lovely help-
mate,—while the eyes of each in this interesting
group were affectionately fixed on his anxious

and disturbed countenance,—he afforded them no glance of kindly regard in return for their sympathy.

" Why does not Mary come home? I like not these evening walks," petulantly exclaimed the impatient father. " Mrs. Lanyon! Mrs. Lanyon! thy precious nephew cannot be far away when Mary is so late abroad. Oh! could I but keep my lamb from that wolf, for wolf he is, although thy sister's son! How have I urged and besought my darling child to give up this unhappy attachment! What prevented her being now the wife of a man of influence, and shining with the proudest even at the court of St. James's? Would she not have been Sir John Godolphin's bride if Trehearne had not crossed her path? And when this, my anxious hope, was given up to her way-wardness, might she not have accepted the addresses of young Stackhouse, who was so devoted to her?"

Lanyon had now talked himself into an un-

governable state of irritability, and would have
been gratified had excuse been afforded him
for further petulance, by Mrs. Lanyon's de-
fending her nephew from his accusations.   All
he had to say was, however, heard in silence
by the patient wife ; and her husband, as if
disappointed at not finding the opposition he
expected, suddenly announced his intention of
seeking his daughter, and, to the temporary
relief of the other members of his family, left
the house.

Trehearne, who will figure as a principal
character in our present narrative, was the
only son of Mrs. Lanyon's sister, the widow
of a commander of an Indiaman, whose death
had left her in circumstances almost approaching to penury.   A cottage near Bostavern
had, with many other kindnesses, been bestowed on her by Lanyon, who though, as we
have represented him, a man of great irritability of temper, was withal possessed of a
warm heart and generous disposition.   Mary

and Trehearne had been playmates till they had become lovers. Lanyon persuaded himself that his wife's praises of her nephew had brought about this consummation, which he at length discovered was anything but desirable; —still, when well-authenticated reports of the wild and disreputable courses of Henry Trehearne, induced his uncle to declare that Mary must no longer consider her former playfellow even as a cousin, there were not wanting those among the old servants of the family who hinted, that their master had led all parties to consider the young people destined for each other.

At the period of which we now write, Trehearne was a tall, handsome young man of about one-and-twenty. Until the age of sixteen, Bostavern had been more his home than even his mother's cottage. Thus Mary, four years his junior, he might have continued to love as a sister, had not the frequent partings and meetings of the cousins within the last five

years of their existence, occasioned by Trehearne's embracing his father's profession,
taught the hearts of each that happiness could
only be experienced when together. It was
during the young sailor's last voyage to the
West Indies, that reports prejudicial to his
character had reached his friends in England.
Trehearne had been always extravagant ; and
many a bill had his uncle taken up for his poor
mother, which her son had thoughtlessly drawn
on her.   But latterly, in place of depending on
family resources, he seemed to have discovered
one of Fortune's short-cuts to wealth ; and several packages had arrived at Bostavern, containing costly presents for each of his relatives,
and even the servants of the establishment were
not forgotten.

As Henry had left the employment of the
ship-owner with whom Mr. Lanyon had first
placed him, little could be traced of his movements on application in that quarter.   All that
the uncle there learned was, that his nephew,

becoming an excellent sailor, had latterly acted in the capacity of mate on board one of their vessels; but, quarrelling with his captain, he had behaved in a mutinous manner, and finally absconded from his ship, stealing the launch, and taking with him several of the most able of the crew, who appeared devoted to him. It was on receiving this information that Mr. Lanyon had thought it necessary to point out to Mary the propriety of combating any interest her cousin might have in her heart, and he then discovered the startling fact that his daughter had already betrothed herself to Trehearne. Though an undefined dread of op-position had induced the lovers to defer making known their engagement till Henry's return, still neither of them looked forward to more decided interference with their attachment than an embargo on their immediate union, and a few lectures on the imprudence of early marriages. Indeed, the intermarriage of cousins was so prevailing a custom in the county of

Cornwall, that such an occurrence seemed in the natural course of events.

Henry and Mary had thus considered what they were pleased to denominate their future happiness as certain ; and it had been agreed, at their last parting, that the young sailor during his next voyage was, by a thorough abandonment of his youthful follies, to regain a character for prudence and economy, that they might with a better grace, on his return, openly declare their betrothal.

When Lanyon took on himself the disagreeable task of making his daughter acquainted with the desperate courses of her cousin, the secret of their love, which, we regret to say, Mary had been the first to propose should be concealed from her father, was, with a burst of tears, confessed. But those tears did not flow for her lover's unworthiness ;—that she did not believe : no ! it was that Henry had been so belied, and her father so harsh in his suspicions. Lanyon's heart ached for his daughter: she was his eldest born, his favourite child. Often had Mrs. Lanyon besought her husband not to show towards Mary that marked partiality which he bestowed on her, even, it appeared, to the exclusion of her brother and sister from a legitimate share of their father's heart. Parents can never too carefully avoid showing a distinction between children in the distribution of their affections. Parental love during infancy and youth should be the patrimony of all, and,—as far as human infirmity will allow,—like the kindly dews of heaven, which descend equally on the " just and on the unjust." The faults of early years should not be visited by a withdrawal of affection from the wayward child, nor should a naturally amiable disposition entitle its possessor to that interest in a parent's heart which excludes others who have the same claim of consanguinity. We, of course, only refer to the commencement of life; for the parental love of after-years assuredly is justly influenced

by the conduct of our offspring. To the in-
experienced in such ties it may appear a task
hard of fulfilment to guard against the froward
behaviour of children influencing our bearing
towards them; yet, strange to say, here is not
the error that so often spreads jealousy and
dissension in families. It is not the natural
yearning of the heart towards the most amiable ;—no, it is the bestowal of our partial
affection on one child in preference to another,
from the accident of sex, or from being the
eldest or the youngest born,—from form or
feature, or the early indications of intellect.
Here the election is made by the father or
mother, often to the ruin of the favourite child ;
and it may be generally remarked that the favoured of a parent under such circumstances
is the first to make that heart ache, the partiality of which was so unjustly engrossed.
This was the case with respect to Mary Lanyon ;—her will had been her father's law until
the eventful epoch in her existence we are re-

cording : her feelings were consequently expressed with uncontrolled violence ; and deeply
did her injudicious parent regret that she had
been so little used to contradiction, as to induce a waywardness likely to involve the most
serious results in after-life.

To prevent his daughter from indulging in
fruitless musings on the early vision of happiness it had been his painful duty to destroy,
Lanyon made her his companion during a short
residence in Truro, a town about twenty miles
distant, where business arising from mining
speculations,—desperate lotteries in which, like
other Cornish landed proprietors, he was too
deeply concerned,—frequently required his attention. In the society where Mary was then
introduced she became an object of deep interest to Sir John Godolphin, a baronet of large
fortune, who had long been pronounced by his
friends a determined bachelor, he having reached his fortieth year in all the single blessedness
of undivided self-love. Miss Lanyon was un-

like the generality of young ladies whom their
mammas had proposed as fit and proper candi-
dates for his hand and fortune; and finding
it quite a relief to seek, after having been
sought till he was wearied, he attached himself
to Mary, whose beauty had greatly attracted
him. Her dejection gave a softness to dark
eyes which shone the more pleasingly from
their subdued expression, and a paleness to a
cheek where the rose was apt to triumph over
the lily,—a redundancy of bloom which the fas-
tidious in female loveliness may yet remark as
giving a hue of " rude health" to the fair natives of our western coasts.

Though Mary rather shunned than encouraged his attentions, Sir John Godolphin
speedily made proposals to her proud and de-
lighted father. Cornwall, even at the present
day, does not boast the appropriation of much
space in those pages so interesting to the parties immediately concerned, yclept the baro-
netage of Great Britain ; and, at the period

we refer to, a baronet within fifty miles of the Landsend was held in greater consideration than we can have the least idea of in the levelling era of 1839. Godolphin, too, was of an old Cornish family, and Lanyon boasted that his forbears had been of Cornwall since the days of the Phœnicians;—Sir John was lord of Wheal Rose, the squire held seven sixteenths of that speculation;—in short, nothing could be more agreeable to each party concerned than the proposed marriage, till Miss Lanyon was taken into their counsels. Here the negotiation ceased: the baronet received a bland but decided refusal; while her father had to endure a renewal of remonstrances and solicitations that plainly exhibited to him his wayward child's determination yet to consider herself the betrothed of her cousin Henry. Lanyon, still fondly indulgent to Mary, urged not her marriage with Sir John Godolphin beyond the expression of parental advice. Finding this had no effect, he returned with her to Bostavern;

his only comfort being derived from Trehearne's lengthened absence, which had now
extended to a period of nearly two years. The
young sailor's letters had informed his uncle
that he was engaged in a very profitable service, though the name of the ship or owner
was never mentioned. Of late his communications had been less frequent, and within the
last four months they had altogether ceased;
thus Lanyon trusted that Henry might have
been the first to prove faithless to the vows of
early love, and that his cousin was forgotten
amid the excitement of his venturous life.

. Mary being now eighteen, her father was
not without expectations that she might yet
marry ere the re-appearance of his nephew.
Shortly after their return to Bostavern, she
received an offer from a quarter where, if worth
and kindliness of disposition could have com-
pensated to the young lady for homeliness of
manner, that prospect of happiness was open to
her, which it has been said is only once dis-

closed in the long pilgrimage of existence : if then neglected,—the vista blending again with the labyrinth of life,—the golden opportunity is past. John Stackhouse was the younger son of a gentleman of moderate fortune ; and, having originally studied for the medical profession, he would have contentedly set himself down as surgeon in a neighbouring town : but the unexpected decease of his father and brother had given him possession of the family estate ; and he resided about a mile from Lanyon in the house of his ancestors, though the payment of his predecessor's debts had sadly thinned the paternal acres.

We have said there was a certain homeliness of address about the doctor, as he was familiarly called by his associates ; but real refinement of mind has not that essential connection with refinement of manners which many suppose. Indeed, both are weighed by a doubtful balance. The man who would betray the confidence of woman, who would wrong his friend,

and squander among sharpers that which he
denies to his just creditors, may be a man
of refined manners. Even the elegant and trifling sensualist, who stoops not to the grosser
vices of the common herd, may be considered
by the superficial observer a man of refined
mind :—but let him gild the temple of his plea-
sures with the meretricious tinsel of fallacious
sentiment ; let passion speak but in the har-
monious numbers of music and poetry, and the
altar of desire be fed with frankincense by the
hand of beauty,—all this but constitutes refinement in sensuality. It has been declared by
the divine, on one hand, that a perfect Christian
must be a gentleman ; and by the philosopher
and moralist, on the other, that the benevolent
man must of necessity be possessed of gentle-
manly feeling ;—and it was on these stable and
sufficient grounds, Stackhouse founded his pa-
tent of gentility.

At the time of which we speak the doctor
was about the age of five-and-twenty; and, in

describing his person, we would say he was a little above the middle height; too sturdily formed to lay claim to elegance,—but in frame, as in mind, possessed of all the requisites for strength and usefulness; while his countenance, though not moulded in beauty of feature, was illumined by eyes beaming kindliness and sincerity. Such was the man who overtook Lanyon on his homeward way, from what in the west of England is termed " a mine account" or settling day, where those interested dine together after the despatch of business. It must be premised that Stackhouse was well acquainted with Mary, and had long regarded her with affection, spite of a waywardness often indulged in by the young lady, incomprehensible to her single-minded admirer; for she had considered the secret of her engagement with her cousin might be endangered by her altogether discouraging Stackhouse's addresses.

" Glad to see you back again amongst us,

squire," cried the doctor, riding up to Lanyon within about a mile of a cross-road that would lead each on a different route to their respective homes.

"It did not seem like it just now, John," replied his friendly neighbour; "or why did you lag behind on the road, man? I missed you at starting, and have walked my horse a foot pace, thinking you would overtake me. You seem to have forgotten that we used to ride home together."

An air of indescribable diffidence threw a shade over the generally open countenance of Stackhouse, as, hesitatingly answering this expostulation, he faltered out, " Yes, yes, I *do* own I did loiter a bit; yet not out of want of love for thee or thine, depend upon it. But I did not wish to overtake you, Lanyon, till I had made up my mind about asking you a question. You have known me from a boy; and, if you know any harm of me, I am sorry for it. The Lanyons and the Stackhouses have always been friends;—they have intermarried before now:” and here the diffident negotiator of a proposal he had so deeply at heart as almost to deprive him of the power of advocating his own cause, allowed his horse to fall a little in the rear of his companion, as though he were inclined to make a retrograde movement in order once more to collect his ideas. Lanyon, however, came to his assistance ere they had quite parted company; and, next to the actual promise of his daughter in marriage, a greater satisfaction he could not have afforded him.

“ Well, John, I think I know what you are going to say. Is it not your intention to be a suitor for Mary’s hand ?”

“ Squire, my dear squire,” cried Stackhouse, again pushing his horse to the front; “ yes, my good friend, it is that I would speak to you about: I hardly knew how to put the question to you;—but is Mary engaged to Henry Trehearne? Till I heard from

Truro the other day that you had encouraged the addresses of Sir John Godolphin, I always feared this was the case; and then putting myself forward in the matter would have been painful to all parties. But tell me now — is Mary free? May I have your good word with her ?"

" I wish I could assure you she was really heart-free, as easily as I can promise you that my good word shall not be wanting," said the sorrowful father. " But Mary has a will of her own in everything. Ride home with me then, and put the question to her yourself;— and, as this will give you courage, I declare to you that never with *my* consent does she marry Trehearne."

Stackhouse suspected, from the distress of his companion, that there was a better understanding between the cousins than was agreeable to Lanyon; but he felt that he had now gone too far to recede; and, having the sanction of her father, he that evening sought an interview with Mary. He found his suspicions correct. She now readily confessed her engagement to Henry Trehearne, with many expressions of regret at having in any way led others to suppose that her hand was disengaged; and, in the end, so deeply interested the kind-hearted and generous Stackhouse in behalf of his rival,—whom she represented, in the confidence of her affection, as most unjustly calumniated,—that, much as he loved her, he actually returned to Mr. Lanyon, not only to withdraw his proposals, but in the vain hope of softening the feelings of the uncle toward his absent nephew.

All Stackhouse urged in this fruitless attempt was listened to with much composure by the old gentleman, till a hint of the possibility of the marriage of the cousins yet taking place,—if Trehearne satisfactorily explained himself on his return,—transported Lanyon beyond all powers of endurance. He had at first felt reluctant to brand the young sailor with the character of a mutineer,—a reckless adventurer whose means of subsistence were too mysterious to be respectable;—but he now forgot all ties of relationship, and completely undeceived Stackhouse with respect to the party whose cause he was advocating, by showing him the correspondence with the ship-owners. Here they actually threatened the apprehension of Trehearne, whenever he came within their reach, for " assaulting his captain, running away with the launch, seducing the crew to break their engagements, and other acts of mutiny and violence."

The doctor was too sober-minded a man not to see that Lanyon had acted prudently in re-solving not to encourage an engagement be-tween the cousins, under the circumstances now disclosed to him ; yet he could not but think it injudicious in the father to bruit the question so strongly before the return of Trehearne, as it only armed the obstinacy of his daughter to oppose the paternal will. It was a matter too delicate for any but immediate relatives to interfere in ; and Stackhouse, though his first impulse of generous feeling had induced him to attempt the negotiation between Mr. Lanyon and Mary,—hoping to insure the happiness of the woman he loved even at the expense of his own,—saw that he had not only espoused a bad cause, but one that he had not the power of advocating without an apparent impertinence not likely to be brooked by his irritable host : Lanyon saying with some asperity of manner, that; when he received him as a suitor to his daughter, he little supposed how very readily he could make her over to another. The old man was so anxious to place his favourite child out of the reach of his lawless nephew, that, in a subsequent interview, he urged Stackhouse to continue his addresses, in the hope that Mary might at length be induced, however reluctantly, to accept him as a husband : but the young doctor withstood the temptation ; and, some trifling business calling him to London, he purposely prolonged his stay in the metropolis,—nor did he return to Cornwall for many months.

Affairs were in this position when Trehearne returned from sea: whatever might have been his career abroad, he imagined not that reports unfavourable to his character had reached Bostavern, which he did not possess sufficient influence with its inmates speciously to explain away. In his mother he knew he had a strenuous advocate, for the widow's heart was in the keeping of her son;—he was the only tie that linked her to the memory of other days. His infancy had been nursed with watchful devotion, which, though a worship of idolatry, seemed to partake of a holy character: in her boy was to live again his father's energies; and,— looking forward to the time when her husband was to be restored in the manhood of his son,— instead of exercising a judicious authority during his childhood, she was only anxious to hasten that period when she might consider herself as looking up to him for protection, if not for guidance and support. Could aught plead in palliation of false indulgence on the part of a parent, it would be, when springing from the influence of feelings such as we have described; but, alas! the young sailor's indiscretions had their rise in the inordinate affection which he now hoped would plead in extenuation of his faults.

The bounding step of boyhood, not yet lost in manhood, had brought Trehearne to his uncle's house, which lay in his route from the port, where he had landed, to his mother's cottage. The latch of the garden-door lifted, and he was again in Mary's favourite parterre; —but no Mary was there to welcome him. He paused but to pluck a rose, his usual morning gift, while a rose was in flower; and he had not forgotten this, though laden then with precious gifts from the Indies, more precious, perhaps, than prudence should have allowed him to purchase,—but they were for Mary Lanyon, and what could be too good for her? Hastening in his approach to the house, he beheld a well-known servant, who appeared sent to meet him: this messenger was Peter, the confidential attendant of Mr. Lanyon; and Henry poured forth a torrent of questions which the old man seemed to find difficulty in answering.

"How is Miss Mary, Peter?—my uncle, my aunt?"

But Peter was charged with an ungracious office; and the old man, who had known Henry from his childhood, at length said,—

"I'm glad to see thee, sure enough, Master Henry; and Miss Mary will be so too, poor young lady! if they'll let her :—but the house is all changed, and is no home for you as it used to be. Not that it's my place to say anything. Master wishes to speak to you in the book-room;—and you needn't try and see Miss Mary, for, directly we heard that you were come home, Master made her keep to her room for fear you should meet."

" For fear I should meet her!" cried Trehearne: " tell me, tell me, Peter, what does all this mean ?"

" Better go and see the squire, sir," was the only reply that could be obtained from the sincerely grieved old man. " Better go and see the squire; I haven't the heart to tell 'ee."

Henry accordingly proceeded to the house, but with what change of feeling from the joyous expectancy of his first approach ! His interview with his uncle was short—indeed, of such a nature, that it was well rendered brief in its duration. Mr. Lanyon reproached Trehearne with duplicity in engaging the affections of his daughter, with an asperity that might have been spared, since only in the concealment of their engagement could blame properly attach to the cousins, so decided had been the sanction given by all parties to an intercourse, the probable result of which was mutual attachment. But, ere Trehearne could remind his uncle of his injustice in this particular, Lanyon hastened to acquaint him with reports bearing unfavourably on his professional career; and concluded by assuring him that Mary must henceforth be as a stranger to one whose character had been so blasted.

This stunning intelligence was at first received by Henry with an apathy that much surprised Mr. Lanyon: the young man made him no answer till he had ceased speaking; but, rising from his chair, stood with his eyes fixed on the speaker, as if he was not exactly aware of the subject in question. This calm lasted but a moment.

" And Mary Lanyon! — what says your daughter, sir, to all this?" slowly and bitterly exclaimed Trehearne, sternly regarding his uncle, who almost quailed beneath his glance.

" She will perform her duty *as* a daughter, I hope ; and you must not persuade her to the contrary, if you would show your gratitude for all I have done for your mother and yourself."

This was said in a half conciliatory tone.

" A curse on your favours, old man !" cried the indignant youth; " they shall be repaid if I pawn my soul for the discharge. Is it now you throw them in my teeth ?—They shall be repaid ! And hear me, Richard Lanyon : if Mary wed any but me, whom she has promised to marry, whom she has loved from a child"— Here choked with passion, or undetermined as to the threat he would pour forth, he rushed from the room, nor ceased running till he found himself at his mother's cottage.

We need not dwell on the agony of the poor widow at so sad a meeting with her son after their long separation. In the evening Mrs. Lanyon visited her sister; Henry heard of Mary, and had the satisfaction of knowing that she was faithful to him,—this his aunt did not deny; but at the same time she assured him that no perseverance on his part could have any effect, as Mr. Lanyon had determined that Mary should never again hold communication with him. Henry had only come into Cornwall for a few days ; he was obliged to proceed to London, where the ship he had for the time engaged in was unlading. This fact he made known to his mother and aunt; and strongly did they advise him to return to his duties immediately, and not fruitlessly attempt to see his cousin. Mrs. Lanyon would even have persuaded her nephew, if possible, to a withdrawal of the claim he seemed to consider he had on her daughter. She appealed to his feelings of gratitude towards her husband, who had been as a father to him,—but all in vain. After much persuasion, Henry at length consented to proceed immediately to London ; but at the same time he solemnly swore, that if Mary Lanyon bestowed her hand on any one save him to whom she was betrothed, his rival's bride she should not long remain.

This undefined threat displeased his aunt and mother, though it did not much alarm them ; from his youth his menaces during

bursts of passion were never followed by determination of purpose in carrying his boyish
vengeance into execution ; Mrs. Trehearne, indeed, always declared him to be too good-hearted
to bear malice : but her son's character had
undergone a severe and awful change,—he was
no longer the violent, impetuous boy his mother
would still have imagined him. Trehearne
had been some years at·sea, and was not only
schooled in the dangers of his profession, but
had become hardened by the scenes in which
he had engaged ; and the reports before mentioned as unfavourable to his character, were
not without good foundation. When in the
employ of the merchants in whose vessel he
had at first sailed, he was more than once in
situations of difficulty that required determination of character, and this quality of mind he
had exhibited in every exigency ; but unfor-
tunately, in the course of the services here alluded to, the young sailor became early initiated in scenes of violence and blood, where the

question of right, which the circumstances of trade induced his captain to advocate to-day, seemed to be forgotten on the morrow, when it was expedient to force the natives of some savage coast to yield points which might not be so fairly demanded.

From such a system, which, we regret to say, is not even now unknown in the South Sea and African trades, the transition was not great, when a quarrel with his commander induced him to take service in a ship changing its character, together with the nature of its enterprise, with every locality,—but which generally proved a Buccaneer whenever a likely prize fell in her 'course.

Trehearne, in apparently following the advice given him by his female relatives, so far as respected his leaving immediately for London, hoped to lull all at Bostavern into a false security. To possess himself of Mary he had fully resolved;—and, only staying in the metropolis long enough to throw up his appointment in his ship, he returned to Cornwall, hiding himself in the neighbourhood of the Landsend amid well-known haunts of his boyhood, where, from thoughtlessness and love of excitement, he had often assisted the daring smuggler to secrete his contraband stores. Here he kept watch on the establishment of his uncle, till he found that Mary was allowed to resume her walks, at first with her father, but at length unattended; Mr. Lanyon considering, from the non-appearance of Henry, that he must have again sailed on some foreign voyage.

We have now brought our reader to the period at which our tale commences, when Mary's lengthened absence had alarmed her father into the belief that Trehearne was not so distant as he could have wished. About to introduce Mary Lanyon in propriâ personâ, we would premise that, our tale being founded on fact, we cannot interest the reader, after the fashion of romance-writers, in a heroine whose peerless beauties were but an index of a faultless mind,—whose frailties arose but from the redundancy of her virtues,—and whose misfortunes, far from being the result of her own conduct, most unjustly had befallen her. Mary was a very pretty girl, it is true; but her dark hazel eyes were frequently lighted up by anger, and her ruby lips were very apt to pout whenever the whole economy of her father's house was not working according to her pleasure. Mr. Lanyon's "dear Mary wishes it, why not indulge her?" was the dictum which influenced her mother, and opposition from any other quarter seemed absolute rebellion. Yet Mary loved her parents tenderly, and doted on her brother and sister; was kind to all the neighbouring poor, not only in the distribution of money, with which she was amply supplied, but showing, by her constant visits and personal attendance in sickness, that she really was sincerely tender-hearted.

Miss Lanyon might have claimed praise for all this, but she was still a self-willed, spoilt girl;

Mr. Lanyon had so long left Mary to her own government, that it was not surprising when, to prevent what he considered would be the actual ruin of her future happiness, he took decided measures to control her inclination, that these were met by an opposition on the part of his daughter, painfully convincing that the love of a spoilt child, however apparently devoted, too often ceases with the injudicious indulgence that called it forth. The plant fostered in the hotbed dies in the genial breeze and shower, from which,—exposed to as a seedling,—it might have drawn vigour::so drooped Mary's affection for her father, the moment she received from him healthful and judicious counsel.

Lanyon, however, was determined to prevent the marriage of his daughter with a man of desperate fortunes,—and such he had good reason to suppose was Trehearne. As Mary would not promise to abstain from all communication with her cousin, she had been confined to her

room as soon as his arrival in England came to
her father's knowledge; but the young sailor's
first visit to Bostavern had passed without the
lovers meeting, and Lanyon began to relax in
a coercion which was almost as painful to
himself as to his daughter. Mary, too, looked
ill; she pined for her usual exercise; and,
during a few walks taken with her father,
contrived to re-establish herself sufficiently in
his confidence to be at length permitted to go
out alone,—her reason for being so desirous of
freedom in this particular, Peter, had he been
disposed, might have informed his master,
he, yielding to her entreaties, having contrived
means of communication between the cousins.

There is a little beach, hidden by the tall
cliffs that tower above its shining sands, near
Bostavern; and here was the trysting-place of
Henry and Mary. A meeting between a love-
lorn youth and maiden admits not of much no-
velty of description. It was but the second time
Lanyon had allowed his daughter to leave

home unattended, and twice had she met Trehearne. The sun was fast sinking beneath the ocean that was spread before them, and yet farewell had not been spoken :—Mary knew that her father must long have been expecting her return ; but still her head rested on her lover's bosom as they sat on the beach, his arm supporting her as she wept. Yes, she was weeping ;—but ever and anon would Henry chide her tears, and, raising her face to meet his ardent gaze, she smiled at his bidding, and then cast herself in his arms to weep again. But though Mary thus yielded to a woman's weakness, who weeps the fault she is committing, there was about Trehearne a sternness and determination which even the sight of Mary's tears could not shake. With an anxious eye he watched the movements of a small rakish-looking craft just rounding one of the points of the bay :—dark clouds were gathering to windward, as if night were impatient at the dying glories of the setting sun, and there was every indication of a coming storm ;—but the hopes of the lovers were in that little bark and rising sea.

Henry had engaged the assistance of a smuggling cutter to carry off Mary to Guernsey. The vessel lay-to, a boat was pushed off, it neared the shore ;—he supported the steps of the still sobbing girl towards a reef of rocks which, running out to sea, formed a natural pier ;—but, ere they reached their place of embarkation, Lanyon appeared on the cliff immediately above them. The agonized father saw with a single glance that the track which would lead him to the beach was too winding in its descent to allow of his getting to the sands ere his daughter would be for ever lost to him. Rushing to the brink of the precipice, his head bared to the wind,—his long, grey hair streaming round features convulsed in the intensity of mental agony, — he called on the ravisher to stop.

" Henry Trehearne !" hoarsely cried the exasperated man, " unhand my child, force her not to leave the shore !—the law shall reach you; though my arm can not." Alas! Alas! he beheld too soon it was with willing steps Mary entered the boat. " My daughter! my daughter !"—the old man lifted up his voice and wept.

But the boat was leaving the shore; and his tears became dried: his arms were again outstretched towards his rebellious child, and amid the roar of the waters, came a father's curse to Mary's ear.

" My curse go with thee, thou unnatural girl! may it sink thee in the waves that now bear thee ;—or, if Heaven spare thee in the coming storm, may thou and thy lover live till love becomes hate! Curse thee! curse thee!"

The old man fell on the brink of the precipice, and in mental agony rolled on the ground, reckless of the peril of the act. That night he returned to Bostavern as one who had bidden farewell to all human sympathies.

When misfortune does not soften the heart to
the dispensations of Providence, it brings on
a fearful state of feeling, too often exemplified
in ill-regulated minds.

Though, yielding to the entreaties of Mrs.
Lanyon, he did not actually cast forth Mrs.
Trehearne from her abode, she was never permitted to visit Bostavern. The endearments
of his wife and remaining children seemed
painful to him;—he tried to devote himself to
business, but he became litigious and irritable
in all his transactions, involving himself in
lawsuits;—and, ere long, by the thorough mis-
management of his affairs, he brought himself to the verge of ruin. Mrs. Lanyon had
watched the proceedings of her husband with
a dread of their result to his family; pious
and long-suffering, possessed of that peace of
mind which " passeth understanding," happily
she could look for comfort that was not of
earth. From Mary she had heard frequently
since she quitted England. Henry had mar-

ried her immediately on their arrival at Guernsey, and she had become the mother of a little girl; but its endearments could not compensate to her for the constant absence of her husband,—now one of the most daring smugglers in the British Channel.

Trehearne was desirous that his mother should reside under his roof, but her constitution, never strong, did not permit of a sea voyage; he therefore contented himself by insisting that she should pay rent for her cottage, nor did he fail to supply her wants abundantly. The gains from his unlawful traffic must have been large; for, after calculating the expenses his parent and himself had caused Lanyon for so many years past, the whole sum was repaid by instalments, which, refused by his uncle, were transmitted to his aunt; who, concealing the fact from her husband, was fain to appropriate the sums thus derived, to her own wants and those of her two remaining children, or the once plentiful board of Bostavern would have been thinly spread.

- Lanyon had been for months absent in London, deeply interested in the proceedings of a chancery suit, about the underground rights of a property sold without reservation, but the deeds of which, he chose to consider, still entitled him to the " lordship" of a mine. The loss of his cause had. ruined him. Lanyon came home almost distracted by the state of his affairs, and found his wife watching the sick beds of his son and daughter by turns, while she was herself suffering from the malady then hastening her only remaining earthly comforts to the grave. A virulent small-pox had broken out in the vicinity, and among its first victims was Mrs. Trehearne, whose sickness and death had been attended by her sister : the consequences proved fatal to the inmates of Bostavern. In a few days, mother and children slept within the same quiet grave in the church-yard of St. Just.

The disease which devastated Lanyon's fa-

mily was too much dreaded in the neighbourhood of Bostavern, where it then raged like a
plague, to admit of that gathering of friends
and kindred usually attendant on a Cornish
funeral. Lanyon, accompanied by Stackhouse,
and followed by his attached Peter, formed the
only mourners. There was that in the eye of
the old man, which alarmed the faithful friend
who supported his wavering steps to the walled
mound that had for ages been the burial-
place of his sires. The light of intellect was
fast departing; while, in its stead, the uncertain
glance which came from beneath his beetling
brows, told that the scene around was but
wildly reflected on the mental retina. The be-
reaved mourner muttered to himself as the
coffins, one by one, were deposited in the
grave; then, turning to Stackhouse, with a
loud voice he exclaimed,—

" Why is not Mary's coffin buried too?—'tis
there! In with it, in with it—deep in the
earth! She caused it all."

Vainly they remonstrated with the wretched

man ; he insisted that the funeral service should not proceed, unless the coffin imaged to his fancy were entombed : nor was the sacred rite concluded until Lanyon had been led, a raving maniac, from the church-yard.

The desolation at Bostavern was unknown to Mary ; but misery has many hands, and she had not escaped their iron grasp. Trehearne, after an absence of some months,—during which time his wife had too much reason to suppose that inclination had greatly to do with his lengthened stay from home,—suddenly returned. After placing at Mary's disposal a small sum of money for the present support of herself and child, he briefly announced his intention of making a distant voyage, that might last some years. She had forsaken all for him ; — the curse of her father still haunted her,— a prophetic curse, the fulfilment of which had commenced,— and *this* was her reward. Trehearne did not communicate his future plans, — the confidence of affection having long ceased ; and the few days that remained ere what they might consider their final separation, were spent in mutual reproaches. That Trehearne's affection had passed away, was but too evident. Woman's love is not so soon extinct; but Mary was not of a disposition to endure patiently the neglect and abandonment of a husband. Their parting was a scene of violence: a blow fell which was shared by the mother and the child; —their blood was mingled, and they became all in all to each other, for the mother ceased to have a husband,—and the child was fatherless.

Mary had little inducement to remain in Guernsey,—she shrank from exhibiting herself as a forsaken wife. It was painful enough to have long appeared cruelly neglected by her husband; for, though nearly broken-hearted, she was still proud. Her thoughts turned towards Bostavern, and, ere she determined on her future place of residence, she resolved once more to see her mother,—not, perhaps, without a latent hope that her father might yet be reconciled to his now miserable and repentant daughter. It was no difficult matter to obtain a passage from Guernsey to Cornwall, but the facility of communication between the coasts was through the medium of smuggling vessels. From one of these Mary was landed with her infant within a walk of Bostavern, on the beach which had witnessed her departure about two years previously. As she gazed upward on the height where her aged father had called Heaven to witness her disobedience,—pouring forth the malediction that seemed still to ring in her ear,—she pressed her unconscious baby to her bosom, and prayed that the sins of the mother might not be visited on the child, as she hurried across the sands, anxious to quit a scene of such bitter recollections.

The evening was fast closing in when Mary reached the gate of Bostavern. Little did she know the changes that had taken place in that once happy home, but the neglected flower-garden told her that all was not right within.

It had ever claimed her mother's care; and a
presage of that parent's illness, perhaps death,
appalled the almost fainting Mary.   Her intention had been to have requested an interview with Mrs. Lanyon; but, though she had
now arrived at a side-door communicating with
the servants' offices, she dared not announce
her coming.   At length, summoning courage,
she knocked gently at an entrance to a kitchen;
— the door, unfastened, swung on its hinges
at her touch, and gave to view a tenantless
apartment, and a cold and cheerless hearth.—
Mary now hoped that the family had removed
to Penzance for the winter season, which was
approaching; and with a lighter heart passed
on to the interior of the house, in the expecta-
tion of finding some one who could give her
the information she desired.   The door of her
father's room was partly open, and her eye
rested on a scene, which for a moment seemed
to entrance the hapless creature, as if she had
gazed on a basilisk;—till, sinking gradually on

the floor, her arms resigned her sleeping child:
—she had fainted.

Before the embers of a peat fire Lanyon
was seated; his hands clasped on his knees,
and his head bowed on his heaving chest.
The mind was evidently wandering, and memory was holding court and revel with madness in the chambers of his brain.   Round
that solitary hearth came the happy faces,
and the jocund laugh, and the song, and
the tale of other days;—but wild and indis-
tinct were these visions of the past to that
old man,—like ghosts of the departed, revi-
siting the mouldering halls their deaths had
made tenantless.

" Mary, my child," with measured accents
exclaimed Lanyon, gently raising his head and
looking inquiringly round,—" Mary, come
here and sing to your old father."

He gazed on vacancy, and no voice was
there to answer him: but the maniac smiled,
and listened;—his head moved as to the cadence

of a song, and his eye was lighted up in his pale face—like a wizard candle in an exhumed skull.

" Go now, my child: see! thy mother beckons thee.—Who said that Mary had abandoned me? The stormy night!—ah! the sea,—the raging sea!"—and up rose the aged man, for his interval of calm was gone.   The scene was changed, but the past was still his present. " Heaven, send thy lightnings! my curse shall ride their blaze!—strike her, ye forked tongues, and speak a father's curse! The boat, the boat!—Robber! restore my child!—No, no, she goes with him; she tramples on her sire, her foot is on my neck!—The sea is lit with flames,—the rolling billows swell with fire. Such be thy fate, rebellious child!"

At this moment, Peter, his watchful attendant, opened the door of an inner apartment, and approached his infuriated master, who, with outstretched arms and eyes dilated, was really enacting a part in the scene his phrensied imagination had conjured up. This faithful servant had obtained such influence over the maniac, that, after being addressed by him in a few words of a stern and decided tone, Lanyon allowed himself to be conducted to the interior chamber.

Mary had not long remained in a state of insensibility, when the cries of her awakened child attracted Peter's attention. The affliction of the attached old man on discovering, in the stranger who seemed dead or dying, his young mistress, we need not describe. Female attendant there was none in the house, and Peter sent a boy to Mr. Stackhouse, while in the mean time he laid the hapless mother on a couch, and did his best to nurse the babe into tranquillity; anxious that his master, whom he had left apparently inclined to sleep, might not be aroused by the cries of the child, and add to the embarrassment of the scene. Greatly to the relief of Peter, Mary was at length restored to sensibility: but oh! with

waking consciousness came the knowledge
that her father was a maniac; and her eager
inquiries for her mother, and brother, and
sister, soon wrung from the reluctant servant the fact of the utter desolation of Bostavern. Ere the arrival of Stackhouse, Mary
had again fainted, and as much needed his
medical care as the solace of friendly sympathy.

Our tale must hasten over the next few
months, during which time Mary was installed
as her father's nurse. This to the repentant
daughter was a painful but a wholesome task.
Lanyon was seldom violent; and though in the
gentle minister to his comforts he did not re-
cognise his child, her attentions seemed to
possess a soothing influence, which enabled her
to be of much assistance to Peter in the charge
which the faithful creature had gratuitously
undertaken. Mary found the support of both
master and servant entirely derived from the
bounty of the generous Stackhouse, whose

respectful solicitude and friendly offices were deeply estimated by the forlorn woman. But considering that, so long as her means allowed, it was as much her duty as her inclination to take on herself the future expenses of her afflicted father, Stackhouse for the present was induced by her to consent, though reluctantly, to such an arrangement.

Mary had been furnished with the address of an agent in London to whom Trehearne had directed her to make application for a further supply of money at the expiration of twelve months after his departure. Before the time expired, it was necessary to draw on this quarter: a letter was accordingly despatched, and an answer anxiously expected. The medium of post communication was slow; but a delay, not easily accounted for on this score, had subjected Mary to much painful meditation as to her future prospects. One evening, when awaiting the arrival of Stackhouse, who had promised to inquire at the nearest post-town if the long-expected letter had arrived, Mary felt more than usually depressed; nor even the endearments of her child, now lisping those early accents so precious to a parent's ear, could win more than a mournful smile from the hapless mother. It was growing late, and the maternal blessing was mingled with bitter tears as the widowed wife laid her child in its little cot, and returned to the window, where she watched for the approach of Stackhouse, whom she at length beheld slowly walking his horse towards the house, as if the tidings he was bringing were those of disappointment.

"No letter again to-day, I suppose," said Mary, meeting the kind doctor at the door; "I see by your sorrowful face that no letter has come?"

"Indeed, Mrs. Trehearne, you have not read my countenance aright," answered Stackhouse gravely, as they proceeded to the usual sitting-room. "It is not the failure of your resources that could make me look so sad; for though these, I candidly tell you, are at an end, this can only give me the satisfaction of providing for the comforts of my old friend and his family, the which, be assured, I am well able to do. No, Mary; you must prepare yourself for more painful intelligence; an affliction which money can neither avert nor alleviate :"—and leading her to a chair he seated himself beside her, and cautiously and gently made her acquainted with the contents of the following letter from the London agent, to whom Stackhouse had written in behalf of Mrs. Trehearne.

" Sir,—In answer to yours of the 2nd ultimo, I have to inform you that the late Henry Trehearne left no effects in my hands. As you do not seem acquainted with the character of the individual you inquire after, I refer you to the public accounts of his trial for resisting a King's vessel in the smuggling cutter ' William,' for which offence he was sentenced to transportation to the colonies. The vessel in which he sailed was wrecked ; and, among the convicts lost, was the party in whom you are interested. There is no doubt on the subject of his death, he having been known to be on board when the vessel went to pieces."

"I am, Sir, &c. &c."

It needed not this intelligence to reveal to Mary that the love of her youth was not ex- tinct, however bitterly it had betrayed her: a twelvemonth had elapsed since her separation from Trehearne, and the spirit of this once proud and imperious woman was now chastened and subdued. The shock she had experienced in the misfortunes of her family had been eagerly embraced by Stackhouse, who was sincerely a Christian, as an opening for the judicious direction of Mary's mind towards the truths and comforts of religion; and though she looked back on the stormy period of her mar-

ried life as on a frightful dream, —commenced in wayward passion and filial rebellion;
ending in satiety, cruelty, and neglect on one
side, and the uncontrolled anger of disappointment on the other; — still, more pleasing
thoughts would sometimes arise. She pictured to herself some blissful period, however
distant, when Henry, once more returned to
England, would again look to her for happiness; — when the fiery love of adventure
quenched by years would have taught him
wisdom : then did she look at her little girl,
and dwell on her infant beauty with delight,
heightened by the hope that a father's eye
might behold it matured in loveliness;—and
many had been her supplications at the throne
of Grace, that Henry might not only return as
a husband to the bosom of his wife, but as a
penitent in the sight of Heaven. Such were
the dreams of happiness which the cold reality,
death, swept from the visioned future of Mary

Trehearne.   Inquiries, immediately instituted
by Stackhouse at the Colonial department, confirmed the fact of her loss; and she was now
indeed a widow, and her child fatherless.

It happened just at this period, that some
mining shares which Stackhouse had purchased,
at their utmost valuation, from Mr. Lanyon,
were unexpectedly productive; and it was an
easy matter to persuade Mary that in equity,
if not in law, the proceeds should be hers.
Thus present exigences were provided for; and
Lanyon, sinking fast into the grave, would want
little more at earthly hands. The only immediate change that threatened the afflicted household was a removal from Bostavern, as, in
consequence of a heavy mortgage being fore-
closed, this property had passed into other
hands. Stackhouse possessed too much real
delicacy to offer his establishment to Mary;—he
being, as well as herself, destitute of female relatives to give sanction to such an arrangement:

— the cottage formerly occupied by Henry Trehearne's mother was thus selected for the future abode of the family.

It was only as a corpse Richard Lanyon left the home of his ancestors. Ere the proposed time of departure arrived, he had resigned his existence. In the hour of death, Reason for a few fleeting moments returned to her ancient seat,—as if to scan the record of the past ere called to give in her account. A short time before the old man died, Mary was summoned to his bedside by Peter, who with broken voice sobbed out, " My master,—my master knows me once again !"

Lanyon had passed the morning of his last day in slumber, and Mary imagined not that a fatal change was so near. It appeared that, when waking from his long sleep, his eyes had opened on his faithful servant. The cold gaze of vacuity was gone :—a smile of intelligence lighted the countenance of the dying man ;—

his lips moved, but no sound came forth; while
an attenuated hand grasped the rough palm of
the honest Peter, whose ear was bent to the
pillow of the bed, hoping to catch the blessed
confirmation of his master's sanity from the
pale lips that seemed trembling to give it utterance. He felt that Mr. Lanyon knew him,
though he spoke not; and with tearful eyes,
raised to Heaven in thankfulness, conveyed the
intelligence to his young mistress. In a moment the daughter was kneeling by her father's
side, scarcely daring to hope that the first act
of returning reason would be forgiveness: he
vainly essayed to speak, but gazed on her as
she wept. His look wore not the character of
inquiry: as if all had been revealed to him,
—her many trials, her repentance, her devoted,
watchful tenderness,—a benign expression stole
over a face on which death was about to set
its seal;—his arms extended, the big tears
rolled down the old man's furrowed cheek, and

Mary was clasped to his bosom. Gently he murmured,—"Bless thee, my daughter!" and the spirit passed away.

The arrival of Stackhouse, for whom Peter had sent, and who now entered the chamber of death, was most opportune. By him Mary was removed from the room, unconscious that her father had spent his latest breath in blessing her. When informed that she was the last of a household where—bitter reflection!—the key-stone of domestic happiness had been displaced by her hand, her agony of feeling was enough of retribution for the past; but we will not intrude on her sorrows. Let us remain with Peter by the corpse of his master. With trembling hand did the old man close the eyes of the revered companion of his boyhood, maturity, and age. Such was often the connexion between master and servant in those days. His affection for Mr. Lanyon was intense: through sixty years of faithful service he might have been said never to have wronged him but once, and this was from love to the darling of his master's heart—to Mary. Carefully and silently did he perform his duties toward the dead, and then took his station beside the corpse; and for the several nights and days preceding the funeral he remained a watcher,—no persuasion could induce him to retire from his post.

" I will serve my master to the last," said Peter; " and when I have followed his honoured body to the grave, then, but not till then, will my work be done."

The fulfilment of the task he had allotted to himself was not permitted him. The morning of the funeral, when the chamber was opened by Stackhouse, though Peter was still found supported in his cushioned chair, the form of the old man was rigid in death, the eye that yet seemed to gaze on the corpse before it was fixed,—the dead watched by the dead!

We will now bid adieu to Cornwall, leaving the house of Bostavern to moulder and decay.

The superstition of the age had banned it with an evil name; and it remained tenantless,—save the owl that built her nest in the ivy of its walls, and the bat which flapped its dusky wing through the deserted chambers.

PART II.

A LIGHT breeze was curling the waters of the little channel running between the coast of the Camaroons and the isolated pirate fortress described in the commencement of our tale. Here a boat, manned by eight rowers, was lying under a cliff of the island, the face of which having been scarped with the greatest care, all trace was obliterated of the track, once giving footing to the native as he climbed from his canoe to the hamlet that crowned the summit of the rock to the westward : as its substitute rope ladders hung from narrow ledges at different heights, which might, on alarm of invasion, be instantly withdrawn, leaving the table-land of the little island inaccessible to a stranger; while, further to dispute a landing, along the brow of the cliff were some eight or ten pieces of ship's ordnance, capable of being depressed almost to the foot of the eminence. It was beneath this formidable height the boat was resting on the gently swelling waves with such apparent security as to mark the character of her crew; they were, indeed, desperadoes from a felucca riding in a bay of the mainland about two miles distant, and awaited the return of their commander, whose real name, Russell, was lost in a cognomen more illustrative of his calling—Blood. He was then receiving instruction for the direction of the expedition now on the eve of commencement; his superior, though for the present incapacitated from sailing with the Fairy, claiming the privilege of scheming the mischief he could not share in.

Thomas Kent, the individual we refer to as being the prime mover in these matters, had been for some time the terror of the African seas. He had two feluccas of a build and appearance exactly similar ; and, each sailing under the same name, seemed possessed of ubiquity.   While one stretched away to the southward,—passed the islands of Princes and Aunabona, and running towards Ascension,—to look for a venture among the homeward-bound Indiamen, the sister vessel was exacting tribute within fifty leagues of the African shores ; and by the time her colleague had taken her round by the Brazils, and—after laying in their turn many an outward-bound India trader alongside, crossing the south Atlantic, was again on the coast,—the second rover was ready to go forth on the same track.   Thus, never seen together, the accounts of their mutual piracies became so confounded with each other, that, had their excesses ever brought on legal proceedings, an alibi in most cases might easily have been insisted on.   The rover that kept the homeward station generally assumed the character of a slaver, and, though looked on with an eye of suspicion by the European factories, boldly entered the ports and rivers of the Guinea coast, collecting information which was ultimately used to the serious injury of mercantile speculation in that quarter.

The rendézvous and depôt at the foot of the Camaroons was unknown to the English and Dutch African companies; and if the French, Spanish, and Portuguese authorities of the coast and islands were better informed on the subject, they had, no doubt for very weighty reasons, lent this nest of desperadoes that secret sanction which yet belongs to the policy of African legislators,—connivance.

The foreign cruiser being supposed by this time on the coast, her colleague was about to visit the southern trades ; but Thomas Kent was unable to take command, having been severely wounded in a late affair with an obstinate Dutch vessel. Though he had ultimately succeeded in ransacking and scuttling his prize,—having previously had the satisfaction of seeing every individual throat cut on board, — and even then was giving audience surrounded by the booty thus obtained; still he cursed his fate in encountering such an ugly craft that would not take the tender mercies of his free trading in good part, without giving him, as receipt in full, a wound that seemed likely to prove a subpœna insuring the rover's speedy appearance at a tribunal where the victims of his many murders would be fearful witnesses against him. Kent's wound, under skilful hands, though dangerous, would, no doubt, have yielded to treatment; but, no surgeon being attached to his island establishment, the ball, which was lodged in the groin, could not be extracted: the hurt would not heal; and a discharge ensued, which, together with the agony endured, induced a prostration of strength, making the tiger of the sea a prisoner in his den.

The roof of the cave wherein he confided to his lieutenant his final instructions, and which was Kent's usual abode when on the island, has now fallen in; but the hollow in which was

comprised its recesses may yet be traced amidst ·
the crags of the western cliffs. Here, stretched
on a couch made from the skins of the African tiger, reclined an athletic form, cast in a
mould of manly proportion and beauty, which
told of power and agility; but the sallow, hollow cheek, and the deep-set and blood-shot
grey eye, looking out from wrinkled folds of
skin tinged with blackness, as if scorched by
the wild fire of its gaze, bespoke that strength
wasting, and that activity fettered by disease.

"You must go without me, Blood,—that's
plain enough, for move I cannot ;—so here you
will find me on your return. Only mind my
instructions as to your course, and I doubt not
you will be able to furnish goods enough for the
South American market; and there will be as
clear accounts in the dealings as if I, Thomas
Kent, was at the helm of affairs,—where I hope
to be next trip."

Blood accepted the outstretched hand of his
captain, and promised obedience to all com-

mands. Folding up the charts which had been referred to in the course of their conference, he had turned to go ; but, as if suddenly recollecting himself, he again faced Kent, who, just then yielding to a paroxysm of pain, writhed with an expression of agony in his countenance his proud spirit ill brooked being witnessed by human eye.

" Why do you not go, sir ?" almost roared the infuriated pirate: " death and the devil! send that black hag from above to me. Who required you to watch me ? I want you neither for nurse nor doctor."

Blood, though a thorough-going villain, had that sort of instinctive love for his captain which may be remarked in bull-dogs, who generally love and follow those most ready to hound them on in their career; thus he bore with patience this abuse, and replied coolly,

" Indeed, Captain Kent, I meant no harm ; I should make a sorry doctor, being more used to make wounds than mend them : but I was just thinking that, if we fell in with a surgeon in any ship we might board, may it not be as well to bring him back with us, in case your hopes of the wound's healing should not come to pass ?"

Actually touched by this mark of consideration in his subordinate, Kent's anger was appeased; and, half apologising for his stern rebuke, he rejoined,

" Thank ye, thank ye,—never mind what I said, Blood; you know I did not mean it. Bring doctor and nurse too, if you like; they may be better than wine or gold to a wretch like me."

He turned his face to the side of the cave, waving his hand in token of dismissal; and Blood, relieving his commander of his presence, lost no time in descending to his boat : — he rejoined his vessel, and, ere the sun had set was standing away to the southward at the rate of seven knots an hour.

No less than four vessels were missing that

season, from which intelligence had been received of safe arrival at the Cape of Good Hope;—but they never reached European port. Without entering into the question how far the agency of the elements or the villany of man were implicated in these losses, we will rejoin the Fairy on her homeward track, which lay in the course of the outward-bound India traders. She had been in chase of a fine and apparently heavily-laden merchant-ship all day, and was coming up with her hand-over-hand, when, towards sunset, the wind died away, and left the two vessels not yet within shot-range; but, though the Fairy could not approach her prey, the fate of her prize was not long delayed. The boats were manned, and, impelled by the lusty stroke of desperadoes ripe for murder and plunder, soon they ran alongside the devoted vessel. We are unwilling to stain our pages with the atrocities enacted during the next half hour, for no resistance was offered by crew or passengers, who, from the first, seemed paralysed by fear ; but, obedient to the brutal hail of Blood, in exultation at some unexpected discovery, let us join a group assembled round the mainmast. A gentleman, in whose countenance was depicted more of anxiety and perplexity, than alarm for personal safety, and a little boy about eight years old, were here subjected to the taunts of a crowd composed of the pirate's crew.

" Found at last, by —— !" cried the laughing Blood, as he exultingly clapped his hand on the shoulder of the elder stranger : " a doctor found for the captain, boys ! I swore he should have one; and it's only cutting his throat, if the brave Kent's on his legs again. But troop, my young master," said he, turning to the boy, who, pale and alarmed, clung to his companion ; " troop, my fine fellow, walk the plank with you, overboard you go!" and dragging the child from the arms of his would-be protector, in another moment he must have shared the general fate of the crew and passengers of that luckless vessel.

"You will not, you cannot be so inhuman!" cried the stranger, as they loosed his grasp on the little fellow: the uplifted cutlass of Blood would in its fall have deprived his chief of the new-found medical attendant, when an appalling shriek arrested every actor in the scene. The head of a cask at the foot of the mainmast burst open; a hand was put forth in supplication; and the staves loosening, gave to view the form of a lady who had been concealed within them. Cramped by having remained long in a confined position, she fell on the deck; but instantly rising, her arms were flung around the stripling whose death had been resolved, as she exclaimed in the accents of despair, "My child! my child! save, save my child!"

"A woman! a woman!" cried the astonished

Blood, pausing in his execution of vengeance on the stranger, and for a moment leaving the boy in the embrace of his mother.

" A woman! a woman!" re-echoed in the patois of almost every European tongue from the crew of the pirate vessel, for that motley multitude was as a congress to which the villains of every country had sent a representative. A wave of Blood's arm, which perhaps was not a little enforced by its wielding in its strength the cutlass before mentioned, stilled the outcry, and arrested the movements of several ruffians, who were about to grasp the hapless female apparently delivered into their hands.

" Avast there, messmates!" cried the commander with horrid imprecations, " the first man that stirs, I'll cut him down ;" and then, trying to laugh the matter off with a rough joke, he said, " D——e, boys! you would not baulk the captain, would you ?—no; let him have the whole lot,—doctor, nurse, and loblolly boy. She's for the captain first, according to rule; and I'll take care that it's attended to." Much more followed in the same strain, but we need not give it record.

After this harangue, by which he succeeded in pacifying the crew, a general plunder of the vessel commenced; she was then scuttled. The lady, gentleman, and child were the only prisoners transferred to the felucca; which, in the course of the night, taking advantage of a light breeze, made sail, leaving her prize to sink with the dead and dying.

The four months' absence of the Fairy had made but little change in the state of the pirate captain, except that, while sickness subdued his frame, his character was losing the sternness which had distinguished it. In place of his former coarse though manly bearing, he was becoming more and more irritable and fretful; added to which, the non-arrival of the cruiser he had long expected to relieve the vessel Blood commanded, goaded him almost to madness. That she was lost, captured, or run away with by her crew, he had but little doubt: nor was he wrong in this last conjecture; for, though the fact never came to his knowledge, the Fairy, a felucca, was one of the pirate vessels destroyed at the island of Madagascar by a combined squadron of the English, Dutch, and Portuguese, in the commencement of the eighteenth century; and, as she was so far off her accustomed track, it is likely she had been cruising on her own account.

"Honest, honest Blood has not forsaken me!" cried Kent, when the appearance of his remaining vessel was announced to him by one of his negroes. This was indeed cheering intelligence to the wounded pirate chief; and he hoped soon to have the satisfaction of hearing a favourable account of her cruise from his lieutenant, who hastened to the island immediately he had brought his ship to anchor.

Kent was still on his couch, looking dreadfully ill, when Blood entered with his prisoners:—need we announce to the reader that now assembled in the cave of the Pirate Island were Mary, Stackhouse, and Henry Trehearne? The recognition was mutual and immediate. The pirate, despite of his wound, sprang upward on his couch, while Mary fell senseless at his feet. Stackhouse stood as if transfixed by the glare of Trehearne's widely distended eyes; and the astonished Blood started aside from the group, and was actually appalled, —perhaps for the first time in his life,—by what he could not but consider a general unaccountable burst of insanity. Trehearne soon recovered himself sufficiently to raise the fallen Mary; his first impulse of suddenly revived though long past feeling was to press her to his heart; but now, assisting to recall her to animation, he beheld Stackhouse. What was his connection with the wife that moment restored to her husband?—unsought, but not unwished for, given back to his arms? How had Trehearne longed, in the many nights of anguish he had lately endured, for the ministering hand of his forsaken Mary to smooth his pillow. Yes, Mary was restored to him; and appealing to the bewildered creature, who was now gazing on his face as if trying to understand the evidence of her senses,—for all appeared to her a strange and awful dream,—he in a voice of thunder cried, " Mary! Mary! who is that man? What has Stackhouse to do with *my* wife? Tell me, or I will destroy him;—destroy you,—myself."

Trehearne raved in the outpouring of uncontrolled passion.

" Listen," said Mary with unnatural calmness, and a solemnity that arrested Stackhouse, who was about to answer the demand of the pirate. "Listen, Trehearne!—We thought you dead—he is my husband !"

With a start, and a long-drawn breath that

sounded through the cave, in an instant Trehearne discharged a pistol at Stackhouse;—the benefactor, the protector, the husband of Mary fell; and its fellow instrument of death was pointed at the hapless woman. Mary spoke not;—crouched at Trehearne's feet, with closed eyes she awaited her doom; and, but that she was a mother, she might have prayed for death. A fair-haired child glided from behind the abutment of a rock; in the disguised stripling before him, Trehearne beheld his daughter. She clung to her mother;— his hand was arrested —the father recognised his child—the pistol fell from his grasp, and he sank back on his couch exhausted by mental and corporeal agony.

Blood had remained inactive during this scene, being too much astounded to take any part in a matter he so little understood; but he now approached Mary, and, with more gentleness than might have been expected, disengaged the girl from her embrace, and would have led them from the cave ; but in a moment Mary escaped from the hand that held her, and knelt by the side of the fallen Stackhouse. His head was raised.—Could she believe that he was not dead ?

" He lives ! he lives !" she exclaimed ; " Trehearne is not his murderer !"

" Who lives?—who calls me murderer?" cried the pirate captain, now but half conscious of the scene before him.

Mary returned to the side of his couch, and pointed to Stackhouse, who, assisted by Blood, had risen, having been only stunned by the pistol-ball, which, in grazing the scalp, had done him but little injury. " Behold him, Trehearne !" cried the powerfully excited woman, " him whom you would have slain,—who gave home and succour to your wife and child when there was none else to aid them ! Trehearne, Trehearne, wife can I never be again to either ; but oh ! wrong not our benefactor, our more than friend."

There was a pause of some continuance: it was first broken by the pirate's requesting the departure of Blood, which was done in a tone that bespoke the mastery of his feelings regained.

" Go your ways, Blood, to the ship; I will hear your report another time;—you see you have brought me old acquaintances. Take yon gentleman with you, and let him be kindly treated in the huts above."

Blood gladly availed himself of permission to depart, and Stackhouse unresistingly accompanied him.

When these two had passed the entrance of the cave, Trehearne,— with any feelings of interest which might agitate either party evidently under control,—deliberately inquired into the particulars of the strange events which had brought about the position in which he found himself with respect to his wife and child. The reader is already acquainted with much that was narrated by Mary: it will be sufficient to add, that, about a twelvemonth after her father's death, Stackhouse offered her the protection of his hand and home; which, feeling as she did the highest esteem for his character, together with her destitute situation, she was induced to accept. They were accordingly married; nor had she, till then, reason to repent the step she had taken. Soon after this event, the mining speculations in which Stackhouse had become involved by Mr. Lanyon proved most ruinous; and at length he was glad to accept a medical appointment at one of our Indian presidencies. It was on his voyage with Mary and her little girl to the scene of his new duties, that the ship in which they had embarked was captured by the Fairy. The disclosures on the part of the pirate were brief, but we must take on ourselves to give the reader a more explanatory detail.

It appeared that it was in consequence of an affair between the smuggler Trehearne commanded and a King's vessel, an offence which he feared might be brought home to him, that he left Guernsey with the intention of joining a ship then fitting out at Liverpool, as it was supposed, for mercantile speculation; but in point of fact she was a piratical vessel, and Trehearne, under the assumed name of Kent, was to have been second officer in this desperate employ. Ere he reached his destination, the information of an accomplice caused his apprehension as one deeply interested in the desperate resistance to the laws, before alluded to. His trial soon came on, which was followed by sentence of transportation. Trehearne had neither money nor consolation to transmit to his injured wife;—from time to time he put off writing, and at length left the country without communicating with her: the vessel in which he sailed was wrecked on the voyage, and he was one of the few who persisted in staying by the ship rather than commit themselves to the boats. The fear of death was overcome by the hope of liberty;—their fetters were cast off;

the crew, their guard, and their gaolers, had quitted them ; they might at least die free. The elements seemed battling around the ship : the breakers howling like sea-wolves about her timbers,—the winds calling to the demon of the storm, demanding their share in the work of destruction, that the waters might not triumph alone ;—while the black rocks combined in fatal wreath beneath the bark,—the lightning struck the reeling masts, and the thunder laughed aloud in seeming triumph. Her keel ground on the rocks—the sea rushed in at her opening seams ; and yet six undaunted men clung to the parting timbers, nor did they yet despair. The wind had by its violence nearly driven the vessel over the reef ; — they had torn off their felons' badges, and—should the ship succeed in clear-ing the breakers—they purposed lashing them-selves to spars, and committing themselves to the waves, ere the wreck was engulphed or went to pieces :—they might thus have a chance of being picked up by some vessel, and with the rescue from death would also come their restoration to liberty.

Such were the dreams of hope during that night of terror. Still beat the waves on the defenceless ship; mast after mast had rolled overboard, when — with a crash that sounded like the rending of an iceberg—the hull broke up, and the fore part of the ship, where the convicts had assembled, falling over into deep seas,—as if some imprisoned monster breathed beneath the waves, down—down in yeasty maelstrom went the wreck. But two survivors rose amid that " hell of waters." They had shared in the dangers of shipwreck before;—they had been long known to each other;—and, if there can be friendship between such men, they were friends. Trehearne and Blood—whom we have already introduced to the reader—clung to the same spar; the rest had perished. Swept along by wind and current, they were by day-break far away from the fatal reef. The weather had begun to moderate; and as the sun threw its arms of light on high, as if in adoration of the God who gave its glories birth, mercy seemed blended with nature's morning sacrifice. Had darkness endured one half hour longer, the ship that rescued them would have passed on her way, unheeding the shipwrecked men she now saved from destruction. This vessel proved to be a Dutchman; and her captain and crew little suspected the desperate characters of the individuals given up to them from the deep. Though their companions in ship-wreck who had taken to the boats arrived safely in port, Trehearne and his associate had succeeded so well in mystifying the fo-reigner into a belief of their having been wrecked in a whaler, that their connection with the convict ship was never traced, and they were consequently supposed to have perished.

After many vicissitudes, the two mariners fell in with the ship Trehearne had originally engaged with at Liverpool; a berth in her was still open to so good a sailor and reckless an adventurer as Thomas Kent (for so we may now denominate him); and in course of time he established himself in the present command, Blood still following his fortunes.

His career after this belongs more to a history of the pirates than to our narrative; enough having been detailed to connect the incidents of our story. The interview between Trehearne and his long forsaken wife was not marked by violent expression of feeling;—much time was passed in mutual explanation,—none in unavailing regret. The future was too dangerous a subject for Mary to trust herself with; and the pirate, though apparently satisfied with all she had disclosed of the past,—and nothing did she conceal,—yet regarded her coldly, as if he feared she might read the secret thoughts that were passing in his breast. On his daughter, however, the unhappy man lavished the fondness of a heart which a long course of crime had not quite

deadened to the yearnings of human sympathy.
Trehearne was indeed broken in spirit and
worn in frame; and though, at times, his
fierce and almost demoniac rage would burst
forth, there were moments when, unseen by
human eye, the pirate wept,—when his troubled
spirit longed to be at rest: but if detected in
such weakness, even by his negro attendants, the
demon was again raised within him, and woe
to the wretch who then crossed his imperious
will! The recognition of his wife under the
protection of Stackhouse had excited his fury
on the instant; but exhaustion of mind and
body succeeded—the storm was past.

After dismissing Mary and her child, he
directed that Stackhouse should be admitted
to him; and, as if communicating with
a stranger, he subjected his wound to in-
spection. The doctor, after deliberate exa-
mination, commenced the extraction of the
ball, which, from its having been gradually
working to the surface, presented no difficult

operation: with it came away a substance that must have either wrapped the bullet, which was fired at close quarters, or have been part of the wounded man's dress; and from this arose the irritability and discharge. Silently did Stackhouse minister to the wretched Trehearne: both as a professional man, and one whose kind heart could not but sympathise in human suffering, he deeply regretted that surgical aid had not been sooner obtained;—the leg was now paralysed, nor could its power be restored, and the once iron constitution of the pirate was completely broken up.

" This should have been attended to before," said the doctor, breaking silence almost unconsciously.

" Likely enough, sir," answered his patient; " yet would it have been prudent, think ye, for Thomas Kent, the rumoured pirate, to have appeared in an African port with the marks of a fray about him, just after the disappearance of the Johanna brig between Whidah and Prince's Island?   But that is not the question now, Mr. Stackhouse," said Trehearne, fixedly regarding the operation of binding up his wound; " what is to be the end of this? Am I to be restored to health, activity, and strength?"

He put the question with an effort of composure which showed how much depended on the answer. " Shall I ever recover strength in that limb, I say?   Shall I ever be aught but a cripple,—a burden to myself and others? I would know the worst, and without reservation."

" If ever you regain health," said the really sympathising Stackhouse, " it can only be by quiet, a perfect repose, and freedom from agitation: as to the limb, I regret to say, nothing can restore it ;—your case has been neglected, and the result must be left to time."

" It is enough," said Trehearne, firmly compressing his lips. " Now leave me ;—your own hurt, I trust, is trifling. I commend those to you whom you have so long protected; let them continue to be your care :—prepare for your departure from the island immediately ; I will consider which European settlement will be your best destination."

On quitting the cave, Stackhouse found Mary and her daughter in one of the African huts. The peculiar position of the former,—a wife of two husbands,—rendered her anxious to return to England with her child, leaving Stackhouse to pursue his voyage to India alone. The husband of her youth, being an escaped convict, could not there rejoin her ; this was not to be desired ;—she only hoped that in some other land he might be restored to society, and abandon his present courses. Stackhouse, though bitterly affected by the prospect of separation from Mary, assented to all she proposed ; but both were desirous, if possible, to change the determination of Trehearne

in sending them immediately from the island.
It seemed their duty to remain, for the present, in the hope of aiding his recovery. Vain
was their application to be permitted to take
on themselves the offices for which they had
been brought to the pirate horde,—Trehearne
refused to see them again. In a few days they
were far on their way to Acra, under the charge
of Blood, and the third night the felucca
lay-to off Cape St. Paul. Ere the pirate
lieutenant returned to the vessel with the boat
in which he had landed his passengers, he
threw a heavy packet to Stackhouse, sullenly
saying, " By the captain's orders ; but d—me
if it isn't hard to throw gold to a land-lubber !"
It contained rouleaus to a large amount, and
the following lines :

" The only barrier to your happiness will
soon be removed.—Existence is a burthen to me.
The pistols I have pointed at your lives will,
ere this reaches you, have done their work :—
their bullets will have met in my brain. I

ask not pardon of man, for I dare not ask it of God,— and I go where human forgiveness matters little. So dies Thomas Kent the Pirate!"

While Stackhouse, Mary, and the little girl were proceeding to the Cape of Good Hope, on their passage to India, the British man-of-war sent against the pirates in the Bay of Amboazes, found their isolated depôt entirely broken up; but the natives from the Camaroon coast told the death of the " White Chief," and a nameless grave was in the cave of the Pirate Island!

END OF THE SECOND VOLUME.

LONDON:
PRINTED BY SAMUEL BENTLEY
Dorset Street, Fleet Street.